60 Quick and Easy Recipes for Home

By: Kelly Johnson

Table of Contents

Breakfast:
- Avocado Toast with Poached Egg
- Greek Yogurt Parfait
- Overnight Oats
- Breakfast Burrito
- Peanut Butter Banana Toast
- Breakfast Quesadilla

Lunch:
- Caprese Salad Sandwich
- Chicken Caesar Wrap
- Mediterranean Quinoa Bowl
- Turkey and Avocado Wrap
- Chicken Caesar Salad Wrap
- Quinoa and Black Bean Burrito Bowl

Dinner:
- One-Pan Lemon Garlic Chicken
- Vegetarian Stir-Fry
- Sesame Ginger Tofu Stir-Fry
- Teriyaki Chicken Stir-Fry
- Caprese Stuffed Chicken Breast

Pasta:
- Quick Tomato Basil Pasta
- Creamy Garlic Parmesan Zoodles
- Pesto Zoodles with Cherry Tomatoes
- One-Pan Chicken Alfredo
- Lemon Garlic Shrimp Pasta
- Pasta Primavera

Seafood:
- Lemon Herb Shrimp Skewers
- Salmon and Asparagus Foil Packets
- Garlic Lemon Shrimp
- Baked Cod with Herbs
- Salmon Salad with Avocado
- Cajun Baked Tilapia

Vegetarian:
- Chickpea and Spinach Curry

- Mushroom and Spinach Quiche
- Cauliflower Rice Stir-Fry
- Chickpea Salad
- Sweet Potato and Black Bean Quesadilla

Soup:

- Tomato Basil Soup
- Lentil Soup
- Butternut Squash Soup
- Quick Minestrone Soup
- Tomato Basil Quinoa Soup
- Coconut Curry Lentil Soup

Salad:

- Greek Salad
- Cucumber and Tomato Salad
- Cobb Salad
- Spinach and Strawberry Salad
- Avocado and Chickpea Salad
- Cucumber and Feta Salad

Side Dish:

- Roasted Brussels Sprouts
- Cauliflower Rice Stir-Fry
- Roasted Sweet Potato Wedges
- Quinoa and Black Bean Stuffed Bell Peppers
- Parmesan Roasted Broccoli
- Sesame Soy Marinated Tofu

Dessert:

- Chia Seed Pudding with Berries
- Fruit Salad with Mint
- Fruit Salsa with Cinnamon Chips
- Chocolate Banana Smoothie
- Apple Nachos
- Greek Yogurt with Honey and Berries

Breakfast:

Avocado Toast with Poached Egg

Ingredients:

- 2 slices whole-grain bread
- 1 ripe avocado
- 2 large eggs
- Salt and black pepper, to taste
- Optional toppings: red pepper flakes, cherry tomatoes, feta cheese, or fresh herbs

Instructions:

Poach the Eggs:
- Bring a pot of water to a simmer. Add a splash of white vinegar (optional) to help the egg whites coagulate. Gently crack the eggs into the simmering water, one at a time. Poach for about 3-4 minutes for a runny yolk or longer if you prefer a firmer yolk.

Prepare the Avocado:
- While the eggs are poaching, cut the avocado in half and scoop the flesh into a bowl. Mash it with a fork until it reaches your desired consistency. Add a pinch of salt and black pepper to taste.

Toast the Bread:
- Toast the slices of whole-grain bread until golden and crispy.

Assemble the Avocado Toast:
- Spread the mashed avocado evenly over the toasted bread slices.

Poached Eggs:
- Carefully lift the poached eggs out of the water with a slotted spoon, allowing any excess water to drain off. Place one poached egg on each slice of avocado toast.

Season and Garnish:
- Sprinkle the poached eggs with a pinch of salt and black pepper. Add any additional toppings you like, such as red pepper flakes, sliced cherry tomatoes, crumbled feta cheese, or fresh herbs.

Serve Immediately:
- Serve the avocado toast with poached egg immediately while the eggs are still warm.

Enjoy:

- Cut into the poached egg, allowing the runny yolk to flow over the creamy avocado and toast. Enjoy your delicious and satisfying avocado toast with a poached egg!

Feel free to customize this recipe with your favorite toppings or additional seasonings. Avocado toast with poached egg is not only tasty but also packed with healthy fats, protein, and fiber, making it a nutritious way to start your day.

Greek Yogurt Parfait

Ingredients:

- 1 cup Greek yogurt (plain or flavored)
- 1/2 cup granola
- 1/2 cup mixed berries (strawberries, blueberries, raspberries)
- 1 tablespoon honey or maple syrup (optional)
- 1 tablespoon chopped nuts (such as almonds or walnuts)
- 1 teaspoon chia seeds (optional)
- Fresh mint leaves for garnish (optional)

Instructions:

Prepare the Yogurt:
- If you're using plain Greek yogurt, you can sweeten it by stirring in honey or maple syrup to taste. Mix well until sweetened evenly.

Assemble the Parfait:
- In a glass or a bowl, start with a layer of Greek yogurt at the bottom.

Add Granola:
- Sprinkle a layer of granola over the yogurt. This adds a crunchy texture and complements the creaminess of the yogurt.

Layer with Berries:
- Add a layer of mixed berries on top of the granola. You can use a variety of berries for a colorful and flavorful parfait.

Repeat Layers:
- Repeat the layers until you reach the top of the glass or bowl. You can customize the thickness of each layer based on your preference.

Top with Nuts and Seeds:
- Sprinkle chopped nuts (such as almonds or walnuts) on the top for added crunch. If desired, add chia seeds for extra nutrition.

Drizzle with Honey (Optional):
- Drizzle honey or maple syrup over the top for a touch of sweetness. This step is optional, especially if your yogurt is already sweetened.

Garnish (Optional):
- Garnish the parfait with fresh mint leaves for a burst of freshness.

Serve Immediately:
- Serve the Greek yogurt parfait immediately to enjoy the contrast of textures and flavors.

Enjoy:

- Grab a spoon and dive into the layers of creamy yogurt, crunchy granola, and juicy berries. Enjoy the delightful combination of tastes and textures in every bite.

Feel free to get creative and customize your Greek yogurt parfait with other fruits, seeds, or toppings you enjoy. This versatile recipe is not only delicious but also a great source of protein, fiber, and essential nutrients.

Overnight Oats

Ingredients:

- 1/2 cup rolled oats
- 1/2 cup milk (dairy or plant-based)
- 1/2 cup Greek yogurt
- 1 tablespoon chia seeds (optional)
- 1 tablespoon honey or maple syrup (optional)
- 1/2 teaspoon vanilla extract
- Pinch of salt
- Toppings of your choice: fresh fruits, nuts, seeds, or nut butter

Instructions:

Combine Ingredients:
- In a jar or airtight container, combine rolled oats, milk, Greek yogurt, chia seeds (if using), honey or maple syrup (if using), vanilla extract, and a pinch of salt.

Mix Well:
- Stir the ingredients well to ensure everything is evenly combined. You can also shake the jar if using a container with a lid.

Refrigerate Overnight:
- Cover the jar or container and refrigerate overnight or for at least 4-6 hours. This allows the oats to soak and absorb the liquid.

Add Toppings:
- The next morning, give the overnight oats a good stir. Add your favorite toppings, such as fresh fruits, nuts, seeds, or a drizzle of nut butter.

Adjust Consistency (Optional):
- If the consistency is too thick, you can add a bit more milk until you reach your desired thickness.

Serve:
- Enjoy your creamy and flavorful overnight oats directly from the jar or transfer them to a bowl.

Tips:

- Flavor Variations: Experiment with different flavor variations by adding ingredients like cinnamon, cocoa powder, or almond extract.

- Fruit Additions: Layer fresh fruits like berries, sliced bananas, or diced mango on top for a burst of natural sweetness.
- Texture: Adjust the texture by adding more or less milk, depending on your preference.
- Make Ahead: Prepare several jars of overnight oats at once for a ready-to-eat breakfast throughout the week.
- Customization: Feel free to customize the recipe to suit your dietary preferences or restrictions. Use dairy-free milk and yogurt for a vegan option.

Overnight oats are not only delicious but also a nutritious way to start your day, providing a good balance of fiber, protein, and healthy fats. They are a versatile canvas for creativity, allowing you to tailor the recipe to your taste preferences.

Breakfast Burrito

Ingredients:

- 2 large eggs
- 1 tablespoon cooking oil
- 1/4 cup diced bell peppers (any color)
- 1/4 cup diced onions
- 1/4 cup diced tomatoes
- 1/4 cup cooked and seasoned black beans
- 1/4 cup shredded cheese (cheddar, Monterey Jack, or your preference)
- 2 large flour tortillas
- Salt and pepper to taste
- Optional toppings: salsa, avocado, sour cream, or hot sauce

Instructions:

Prepare Ingredients:
- Chop the bell peppers, onions, and tomatoes. Ensure that all ingredients are ready to go before you start cooking.

Cook Vegetables:
- In a skillet over medium heat, add cooking oil. Sauté the diced bell peppers and onions until they are softened and slightly caramelized.

Scramble Eggs:
- Push the sautéed vegetables to one side of the skillet. Crack the eggs into the skillet and scramble them. Season with salt and pepper.

Combine Ingredients:
- Once the eggs are almost fully cooked, mix them with the sautéed vegetables. Add diced tomatoes and cooked black beans. Stir until everything is well combined.

Warm Tortillas:
- In a separate skillet or directly on a gas flame, warm the flour tortillas until they are pliable.

Assemble Burritos:
- Spoon the egg and vegetable mixture onto the center of each tortilla. Sprinkle shredded cheese on top.

Fold and Roll:
- Fold in the sides of the tortilla and then roll it up from the bottom to create a burrito.

Optional: Toast (Optional):

- If you prefer a slightly crispy texture, you can toast the assembled burritos in a skillet or oven for a few minutes.

Add Toppings:
- Garnish the breakfast burrito with your favorite toppings, such as salsa, sliced avocado, sour cream, or hot sauce.

Serve:
- Place the breakfast burritos on a plate, seam side down. Cut them in half diagonally if desired and serve immediately.

Tips:

- Protein Options: Add cooked bacon, sausage, or ham for additional protein.
- Vegetarian Option: Make it vegetarian by omitting meat and adding extra veggies or plant-based protein alternatives.
- Make-Ahead: Prepare the filling in advance and assemble the burritos when you're ready to eat.
- Customization: Customize the recipe based on your preferences and spice tolerance.

This breakfast burrito recipe is versatile, allowing you to get creative with your favorite ingredients. It's a portable and flavorful breakfast option that provides a good balance of protein, vegetables, and carbohydrates to kickstart your day.

Peanut Butter Banana Toast

Ingredients:

- 2 slices whole-grain bread
- 2 tablespoons peanut butter (smooth or crunchy)
- 1 large ripe banana, thinly sliced
- Honey or maple syrup (optional)
- Chia seeds or sliced almonds (optional)

Instructions:

Toast the Bread:
- Toast the slices of whole-grain bread to your desired level of crispiness.

Spread Peanut Butter:
- While the bread is still warm, spread a generous layer of peanut butter on each slice.

Add Sliced Banana:
- Place the thinly sliced banana evenly over the peanut butter.

Drizzle with Honey (Optional):
- If you desire extra sweetness, drizzle honey or maple syrup over the top.

Optional Toppings:
- Sprinkle chia seeds or sliced almonds for added texture and nutrition.

Serve Immediately:
- Serve the Peanut Butter Banana Toast immediately while the toast is warm and the banana is fresh.

Enjoy:
- Grab a slice, take a bite, and enjoy the delightful combination of creamy peanut butter, sweet banana, and the crunch of the toast.

Variations:

- Nutella Twist: Instead of peanut butter, spread Nutella on the toast for a chocolatey twist.
- Berry Bliss: Add a handful of fresh berries or sliced strawberries on top of the banana for a burst of fruity flavor.
- Protein Boost: Sprinkle with chia seeds, sliced almonds, or hemp seeds for an extra protein boost.
- Cinnamon Spice: Sprinkle a pinch of ground cinnamon on top for a warm and aromatic flavor.

This Peanut Butter Banana Toast is not only delicious but also a great source of energy with the combination of complex carbohydrates, healthy fats, and natural sugars. It makes for a quick and satisfying breakfast or snack that you can prepare in minutes.

Breakfast Quesadilla

Ingredients:

- 2 large eggs
- 2 large flour tortillas
- 1/2 cup shredded cheese (cheddar, Monterey Jack, or your preference)
- 1/4 cup diced bell peppers (any color)
- 1/4 cup diced onions
- 1/4 cup diced tomatoes
- 2 slices cooked bacon or sausage (optional)
- Salt and pepper to taste
- Cooking oil or butter for the pan
- Salsa, sour cream, or guacamole for serving (optional)

Instructions:

Prepare Ingredients:
- Dice the bell peppers, onions, tomatoes, and any additional ingredients you'd like to add.

Cook Eggs:
- In a bowl, beat the eggs and season with salt and pepper. Scramble the eggs in a pan over medium heat until just set.

Assemble Quesadilla:
- Place a tortilla on a flat surface. Sprinkle half of the shredded cheese evenly over one half of the tortilla.

Add Fillings:
- Layer the cooked scrambled eggs, diced bell peppers, onions, tomatoes, and any optional ingredients (bacon or sausage) over the cheese.

Top with More Cheese:
- Sprinkle the remaining half of the shredded cheese on top of the fillings.

Fold and Cook:
- Fold the tortilla in half, pressing it gently to hold the ingredients together. Heat a pan over medium heat and add a bit of cooking oil or butter.

Cook Quesadilla:
- Place the folded quesadilla in the pan and cook for 2-3 minutes on each side or until the tortilla is golden brown and the cheese is melted.

Repeat (Optional):
- If making multiple quesadillas, repeat the process for each one.

Slice and Serve:

- Once cooked, transfer the quesadilla to a cutting board and let it rest for a moment. Slice it into wedges.

Serve with Toppings:
- Serve the breakfast quesadilla with your choice of toppings, such as salsa, sour cream, or guacamole.

Tips:

- Customization: Feel free to customize the filling with ingredients like avocado, black beans, or different types of cheese.
- Spice it Up: Add a pinch of cayenne pepper, hot sauce, or salsa for an extra kick.
- Make it Ahead: Prepare the scrambled eggs and chop the vegetables ahead of time for a quicker assembly in the morning.

This breakfast quesadilla is versatile and can be adapted to suit your taste preferences.

It's a portable and delicious way to enjoy a savory breakfast with a Mexican twist.

Lunch:
Caprese Salad Sandwich

Ingredients:

Fresh mozzarella cheese, sliced
Ripe tomatoes, sliced
Fresh basil leaves
Good quality bread (baguette, ciabatta, or any bread of your choice)
Extra virgin olive oil
Balsamic glaze (optional)
Salt and pepper to taste

Instructions:

Prepare the Ingredients:
- Slice the fresh mozzarella cheese and ripe tomatoes into even slices.
- Wash and dry fresh basil leaves.

Assemble the Sandwich:
- Lay out the slices of bread on a clean surface.
- On one slice, layer the fresh mozzarella slices.
- On another slice, place the tomato slices.
- Add fresh basil leaves on top of the tomatoes.
- Drizzle with extra virgin olive oil.
- Optionally, add a drizzle of balsamic glaze for extra flavor.
- Sprinkle with salt and pepper to taste.

Combine and Serve:
- Place the mozzarella-topped slice over the tomato-basil-topped slice to create a sandwich.
- Press the sandwich gently together.

Optional Grilling:
- If you prefer a warm sandwich, you can grill it on a panini press or in a skillet until the cheese is melted, and the bread is toasted.

Slice and Enjoy:
- Once the sandwich is assembled and grilled (if desired), slice it diagonally or in half.
- Serve immediately and enjoy your delicious Caprese Salad Sandwich.

Feel free to customize the sandwich based on your preferences. You can add additional ingredients like pesto, roasted red peppers, or avocado for extra flavor. The key is to use fresh, high-quality ingredients to capture the essence of a classic Caprese salad in sandwich form.

Chicken Caesar Wrap

Ingredients:

    Grilled or cooked chicken breast, sliced
    Romaine lettuce, chopped
    Caesar dressing
    Parmesan cheese, grated
    Cherry tomatoes, halved
    Flour tortillas or whole-grain wraps

Instructions:

Prepare the Chicken:
- Grill or cook the chicken breast until fully cooked.
- Slice the chicken breast into thin strips.

Assemble the Wrap:
- Lay out a tortilla or wrap on a clean surface.
- Place a handful of chopped Romaine lettuce in the center of the tortilla.

Add Chicken and Toppings:
- Arrange the sliced grilled chicken on top of the lettuce.
- Sprinkle grated Parmesan cheese over the chicken.
- Add halved cherry tomatoes to the wrap.

Drizzle with Caesar Dressing:
- Drizzle Caesar dressing over the ingredients. Use as much or as little as you prefer, depending on your taste.

Wrap It Up:
- Fold in the sides of the tortilla and then roll it up tightly from the bottom, creating a wrap.

Slice and Serve:
- If desired, you can slice the wrap diagonally for easier handling and presentation.
- Serve immediately, and enjoy your Chicken Caesar Wrap.

Feel free to customize the wrap by adding croutons, bacon bits, or extra vegetables like cucumbers or red onions for additional texture and flavor. This recipe is versatile, and you can adapt it to suit your preferences. It's a perfect option for a quick and satisfying lunch or dinner.

Mediterranean Quinoa Bowl

Ingredients:

For the Quinoa:

    1 cup quinoa, rinsed
    2 cups water or vegetable broth
    Salt to taste

For the Bowl:

4. Cherry tomatoes, halved

    Cucumber, diced
    Kalamata olives, pitted and sliced
    Red onion, finely chopped
    Feta cheese, crumbled
    Fresh parsley, chopped
    Extra virgin olive oil
    Lemon juice
    Salt and pepper to taste
    Optional: Hummus for serving

Instructions:

Cook the Quinoa:
- Rinse the quinoa under cold water.
- In a saucepan, combine quinoa and water or vegetable broth.
- Bring to a boil, then reduce heat to low, cover, and simmer for about 15 minutes or until the quinoa is cooked and water is absorbed.
- Fluff the quinoa with a fork and season with salt to taste.

Prepare the Mediterranean Ingredients:
- While the quinoa is cooking, chop the cherry tomatoes, cucumber, olives, red onion, and parsley.
- Crumble the feta cheese.

Assemble the Quinoa Bowl:
- In serving bowls, layer the cooked quinoa as the base.
- Arrange the cherry tomatoes, cucumber, olives, red onion, and crumbled feta on top of the quinoa.

Dress the Bowl:
- Drizzle extra virgin olive oil and lemon juice over the ingredients.
- Season with salt and pepper to taste.
- Toss gently to combine all the flavors.

Garnish and Serve:
- Sprinkle chopped fresh parsley over the bowl.
- Optionally, add a dollop of hummus on the side for extra creaminess.

Enjoy:
- Serve immediately and enjoy your Mediterranean Quinoa Bowl.

Feel free to customize your bowl by adding ingredients like roasted red peppers, artichoke hearts, or grilled chicken for additional protein. This dish is not only delicious but also a great option for a wholesome and satisfying meal.

Turkey and Avocado Wrap

Ingredients:

Tortillas or wraps (whole wheat or your preferred type)
Sliced turkey breast (pre-cooked or deli-sliced)
Ripe avocado, sliced
Lettuce leaves (e.g., romaine or iceberg)
Tomato, sliced
Red onion, thinly sliced
Mayonnaise or your favorite dressing
Mustard (optional)
Salt and pepper to taste

Instructions:

Prepare the Ingredients:
- Slice the turkey breast, avocado, tomato, and red onion.

Warm the Tortillas:
- If you prefer, you can warm the tortillas in a dry skillet or microwave for a few seconds to make them more pliable.

Assemble the Wrap:
- Lay out a tortilla on a clean surface.

Layer the Ingredients:
- Place a few slices of turkey evenly across the center of the tortilla.
- Add sliced avocado on top of the turkey.
- Layer lettuce leaves, tomato slices, and red onion.

Dress the Wrap:
- Drizzle mayonnaise or your favorite dressing over the ingredients.
- Optionally, add mustard for extra flavor.
- Sprinkle salt and pepper to taste.

Wrap It Up:
- Fold in the sides of the tortilla and then roll it up tightly from the bottom, creating a wrap.

Slice and Serve:
- If desired, you can slice the wrap diagonally for easier handling.
- Serve immediately, and enjoy your Turkey and Avocado Wrap.

Feel free to customize your wrap by adding ingredients like bacon, cheese, or sprouts. This versatile recipe allows you to tailor it to your taste preferences. It's a quick and nutritious option for a meal on the go.

Chicken Caesar Salad Wrap

Ingredients:

- Grilled or cooked chicken breast, sliced
- Romaine lettuce, chopped
- Caesar dressing
- Parmesan cheese, grated
- Cherry tomatoes, halved
- Flour tortillas or whole-grain wraps

Instructions:

Prepare the Chicken:
- Grill or cook the chicken breast until fully cooked.
- Slice the chicken breast into thin strips.

Assemble the Wrap:
- Lay out a tortilla or wrap on a clean surface.
- Spread a layer of chopped Romaine lettuce in the center of the tortilla.

Add Chicken and Toppings:
- Place the sliced grilled chicken on top of the lettuce.
- Sprinkle grated Parmesan cheese over the chicken.
- Add halved cherry tomatoes to the wrap.

Drizzle with Caesar Dressing:
- Drizzle Caesar dressing over the ingredients. Use as much or as little as you prefer, depending on your taste.

Wrap It Up:
- Fold in the sides of the tortilla and then roll it up tightly from the bottom, creating a wrap.

Slice and Serve:
- If desired, you can slice the wrap diagonally for easier handling and presentation.
- Serve immediately, and enjoy your Chicken Caesar Salad Wrap.

Feel free to customize the wrap by adding croutons, bacon bits, or additional vegetables for extra crunch and flavor. This recipe is flexible, allowing you to adjust it according to your preferences. It's a great option for a quick and satisfying lunch or dinner.

Quinoa and Black Bean Burrito Bowl

Ingredients:

For the Quinoa:

- 1 cup quinoa, rinsed
- 2 cups vegetable broth or water
- 1 teaspoon cumin
- Salt to taste

For the Black Beans:

5. 1 can (15 oz) black beans, drained and rinsed

- 1 teaspoon ground cumin
- 1 teaspoon chili powder
- Salt to taste

For the Bowl:

9. Corn kernels (fresh, canned, or frozen)

- Avocado, sliced
- Cherry tomatoes, halved
- Red onion, finely chopped
- Fresh cilantro, chopped
- Lime wedges
- Optional toppings: salsa, Greek yogurt or sour cream, shredded cheese

Instructions:

Cook the Quinoa:
- In a saucepan, combine quinoa, vegetable broth or water, cumin, and salt.
- Bring to a boil, then reduce heat to low, cover, and simmer for about 15 minutes or until quinoa is cooked and liquid is absorbed.
- Fluff quinoa with a fork and set aside.

Prepare the Black Beans:
- In a separate saucepan, heat the black beans over medium heat.
- Add ground cumin, chili powder, and salt.

- Stir occasionally until the beans are heated through and the spices are well combined. Set aside.

Assemble the Burrito Bowl:
- In serving bowls, layer the cooked quinoa and seasoned black beans.

Add Toppings:
- Top the quinoa and black beans with corn kernels, sliced avocado, cherry tomatoes, chopped red onion, and fresh cilantro.

Squeeze Lime and Add Optional Toppings:
- Squeeze fresh lime juice over the bowl for added brightness.
- Optionally, add salsa, Greek yogurt or sour cream, and shredded cheese as desired.

Serve and Enjoy:
- Toss the ingredients gently to combine flavors.
- Serve the Quinoa and Black Bean Burrito Bowl immediately, allowing everyone to customize their bowl with additional toppings.

This burrito bowl is not only delicious but also packed with nutrients and customizable to suit your preferences. It's a great vegetarian option and can be easily adapted to include meat or other ingredients based on your taste.

Dinner:
One-Pan Lemon Garlic Chicken

Ingredients:

    4 boneless, skinless chicken breasts
    4 tablespoons olive oil
    4 cloves garlic, minced
    1 teaspoon dried oregano
    1 teaspoon dried thyme
    1 teaspoon paprika
    Salt and pepper to taste
    Zest and juice of 1 lemon
    1 cup chicken broth
    Fresh parsley, chopped (for garnish)

Instructions:

Preheat the Oven:
- Preheat your oven to 400°F (200°C).

Season the Chicken:
- Pat the chicken breasts dry with paper towels.
- In a small bowl, mix together the dried oregano, thyme, paprika, minced garlic, salt, and pepper.
- Rub the chicken breasts with the spice mixture, ensuring they are well coated.

Sear the Chicken:
- In an oven-safe skillet or pan, heat olive oil over medium-high heat.
- Add the seasoned chicken breasts to the hot pan and sear them for 2-3 minutes on each side until golden brown.

Add Lemon and Broth:
- Add the lemon zest and lemon juice to the pan.
- Pour in the chicken broth around the chicken breasts.

Bake in the Oven:
- Transfer the skillet to the preheated oven and bake for about 20-25 minutes or until the chicken is cooked through, and the internal temperature reaches 165°F (74°C).

Garnish and Serve:

- Once the chicken is cooked, remove the pan from the oven.
- Garnish the chicken with fresh chopped parsley.
- Serve the One-Pan Lemon Garlic Chicken with your favorite side dishes, such as roasted vegetables, rice, or a salad.

This dish is not only delicious but also incredibly convenient with minimal cleanup. The lemon and garlic add brightness and flavor to the chicken, making it a perfect option for a quick and tasty meal.

Vegetarian Stir-Fry

Ingredients:

For the Stir-Fry Sauce:

    3 tablespoons soy sauce
    2 tablespoons hoisin sauce
    1 tablespoon rice vinegar
    1 tablespoon sesame oil
    1 tablespoon cornstarch
    1 tablespoon water
    1 teaspoon sugar (optional)

For the Stir-Fry:

8. 2 tablespoons vegetable oil (for cooking)

    1 block extra-firm tofu, pressed and cubed (or your preferred protein substitute)
    4 cups mixed vegetables (broccoli, bell peppers, snap peas, carrots, mushrooms, etc.), sliced or chopped
    3 cloves garlic, minced
    1 tablespoon ginger, grated
    Cooked rice or noodles for serving

Instructions:

Prepare the Stir-Fry Sauce:

    In a small bowl, whisk together soy sauce, hoisin sauce, rice vinegar, sesame oil, cornstarch, water, and sugar (if using). Set aside.

Cook the Tofu (or Protein Substitute):

2. Heat 1 tablespoon of vegetable oil in a large skillet or wok over medium-high heat.

Add the cubed tofu to the pan and cook until all sides are golden brown. If using another protein substitute, cook it according to package instructions.
Remove the tofu from the pan and set it aside.

Prepare the Vegetables:

5. In the same pan, add another tablespoon of oil if needed.

Add minced garlic and grated ginger to the pan, and stir for about 30 seconds until fragrant.
Add the mixed vegetables to the pan and stir-fry for 3-5 minutes or until they are slightly tender but still crisp.

Combine Tofu and Vegetables:

8. Return the cooked tofu to the pan with the vegetables.

Add Stir-Fry Sauce:

9. Pour the prepared stir-fry sauce over the tofu and vegetables.

Stir well to coat everything evenly and let it cook for an additional 2-3 minutes until the sauce thickens.

Serve:

11. Serve the vegetarian stir-fry over cooked rice or noodles.

Feel free to customize the recipe by adding your favorite vegetables or adjusting the level of spice. This vegetarian stir-fry is a quick and nutritious meal that can be easily adapted to suit your taste preferences.

Sesame Ginger Tofu Stir-Fry

Ingredients:

For the Sauce:

- 3 tablespoons soy sauce
- 2 tablespoons sesame oil
- 1 tablespoon rice vinegar
- 1 tablespoon maple syrup or honey
- 1 tablespoon fresh ginger, grated
- 2 cloves garlic, minced
- 1 teaspoon cornstarch

For the Stir-Fry:

8. 1 block extra-firm tofu, pressed and cubed

- 2 tablespoons vegetable oil (for cooking)
- 4 cups mixed vegetables (broccoli, bell peppers, snap peas, carrots, etc.), sliced or chopped
- 2 tablespoons sesame seeds (for garnish)
- Green onions, chopped (for garnish)
- Cooked rice or noodles for serving

Instructions:

Prepare the Sauce:

In a small bowl, whisk together soy sauce, sesame oil, rice vinegar, maple syrup or honey, grated ginger, minced garlic, and cornstarch. Set aside.

Cook the Tofu:

2. Heat 1 tablespoon of vegetable oil in a large skillet or wok over medium-high heat.

Add the cubed tofu to the pan and cook until all sides are golden brown. Remove the tofu from the pan and set it aside.

Stir-Fry the Vegetables:

5. In the same pan, add another tablespoon of oil if needed.

>Add the mixed vegetables to the pan and stir-fry for 3-5 minutes or until they are slightly tender but still crisp.

Combine Tofu and Vegetables:

7. Return the cooked tofu to the pan with the vegetables.

Add Sauce:

8. Pour the prepared sesame ginger sauce over the tofu and vegetables.

>Stir well to coat everything evenly and let it cook for an additional 2-3 minutes until the sauce thickens.

Garnish and Serve:

10. Sprinkle sesame seeds and chopped green onions over the stir-fry.

>Serve the Sesame Ginger Tofu Stir-Fry over cooked rice or noodles.

Feel free to customize the recipe by adding more vegetables or adjusting the sweetness and spiciness of the sauce according to your taste. This flavorful stir-fry is a great way to enjoy the richness of sesame and the warmth of ginger in a wholesome, plant-based meal.

Teriyaki Chicken Stir-Fry

Ingredients:

For the Teriyaki Sauce:

- 1/2 cup soy sauce
- 3 tablespoons mirin (Japanese sweet rice wine) or dry sherry
- 3 tablespoons honey or maple syrup
- 1 tablespoon rice vinegar
- 1 teaspoon sesame oil
- 1 teaspoon ginger, grated
- 2 cloves garlic, minced
- 1 tablespoon cornstarch mixed with 2 tablespoons water (for thickening)

For the Stir-Fry:

9. 1 lb (450g) boneless, skinless chicken breasts or thighs, thinly sliced

- 2 tablespoons vegetable oil
- 4 cups mixed vegetables (broccoli, bell peppers, carrots, snap peas, etc.), sliced or chopped
- Cooked rice for serving
- Sesame seeds and green onions for garnish (optional)

Instructions:

Prepare the Teriyaki Sauce:

In a bowl, whisk together soy sauce, mirin or sherry, honey or maple syrup, rice vinegar, sesame oil, grated ginger, and minced garlic.
Heat the mixture in a saucepan over medium heat. Bring it to a simmer.
In a small bowl, mix cornstarch with water to create a slurry. Add the slurry to the saucepan, stirring constantly until the sauce thickens. Remove from heat and set aside.

Cook the Chicken:

4. Heat 1 tablespoon of vegetable oil in a large skillet or wok over medium-high heat.

Add the sliced chicken to the pan and cook until browned and cooked through. Once the chicken is cooked, remove it from the pan and set it aside.

Stir-Fry the Vegetables:

7. In the same pan, add another tablespoon of oil if needed.

Add the mixed vegetables to the pan and stir-fry for 3-5 minutes or until they are slightly tender but still crisp.

Combine Chicken and Vegetables:

9. Return the cooked chicken to the pan with the vegetables.

Add Teriyaki Sauce:

10. Pour the prepared teriyaki sauce over the chicken and vegetables.

Stir well to coat everything evenly and let it cook for an additional 2-3 minutes until the sauce thickens and coats the chicken and vegetables.

Serve:

12. Serve the Teriyaki Chicken Stir-Fry over cooked rice.

Garnish with sesame seeds and chopped green onions if desired.

Feel free to customize the recipe by adding your favorite vegetables or adjusting the sweetness and saltiness of the teriyaki sauce according to your taste. This flavorful stir-fry is a delightful way to enjoy a classic Japanese-inspired dish at home.

Caprese Stuffed Chicken Breast

Ingredients:

    4 boneless, skinless chicken breasts
    Salt and pepper to taste
    4 ounces fresh mozzarella cheese, sliced
    2 large tomatoes, sliced
    Fresh basil leaves
    2 tablespoons balsamic glaze
    Olive oil for drizzling (optional)
    Toothpicks or kitchen twine (for securing the chicken)

Instructions:

    Preheat the Oven:
- Preheat your oven to 375°F (190°C).

    Prepare the Chicken:
- Lay each chicken breast flat on a cutting board. Use a sharp knife to carefully make a horizontal slit along the side of each chicken breast, creating a pocket for the stuffing.
- Season the inside and outside of each chicken breast with salt and pepper.

    Stuff the Chicken:
- Stuff each chicken breast with slices of fresh mozzarella, tomato, and fresh basil leaves. Try to distribute the stuffing ingredients evenly.

    Secure the Chicken:
- Use toothpicks or kitchen twine to secure the opening of each stuffed chicken breast, ensuring that the stuffing stays inside.

    Season and Drizzle:
- Place the stuffed and secured chicken breasts on a baking sheet or in a baking dish.
- Drizzle olive oil over the top of each chicken breast (optional) and season with additional salt and pepper if desired.

    Bake in the Oven:
- Bake in the preheated oven for about 25-30 minutes or until the chicken is cooked through and no longer pink in the center.

    Broil (Optional):

- If you'd like a golden-brown crust on the top, you can broil the chicken for an additional 2-3 minutes at the end.

Serve with Balsamic Glaze:
- Once the chicken is cooked, drizzle balsamic glaze over each stuffed chicken breast before serving.

Garnish and Enjoy:
- Garnish with additional fresh basil leaves and serve the Caprese Stuffed Chicken Breast with your favorite side dishes.

This dish captures the freshness of a Caprese salad within a succulent chicken breast, making it a delightful and visually appealing meal.

Pasta:
Quick Tomato Basil Pasta

Ingredients:

8 ounces (about 225g) of your favorite pasta (spaghetti, penne, or any shape you prefer)
2 tablespoons olive oil
3 cloves garlic, minced
1 can (14 ounces) crushed tomatoes
Salt and black pepper to taste
Crushed red pepper flakes (optional, for heat)
Fresh basil leaves, chopped
Grated Parmesan cheese for serving

Instructions:

Cook the Pasta:
- Cook the pasta according to the package instructions in a large pot of salted boiling water until al dente. Reserve about 1/2 cup of pasta cooking water before draining.

Prepare the Sauce:
- While the pasta is cooking, heat olive oil in a large skillet over medium heat.
- Add minced garlic and sauté for about 1-2 minutes until fragrant, being careful not to burn it.

Add Crushed Tomatoes:
- Pour the crushed tomatoes into the skillet. Season with salt, black pepper, and crushed red pepper flakes (if using). Stir to combine.

Simmer the Sauce:
- Allow the tomato sauce to simmer for 8-10 minutes, stirring occasionally, until it thickens slightly.

Combine Pasta and Sauce:
- Add the cooked and drained pasta to the skillet with the tomato sauce. Toss the pasta in the sauce until well-coated. If needed, add a bit of the reserved pasta cooking water to reach your desired consistency.

Add Fresh Basil:
- Stir in the chopped fresh basil, reserving some for garnish.

Serve:
- Serve the quick tomato basil pasta in individual bowls, garnished with additional fresh basil and grated Parmesan cheese.

This recipe is versatile, and you can customize it by adding extras like cherry tomatoes, olives, or capers for additional flavor. It's a perfect go-to recipe for a satisfying and speedy pasta dinner.

Creamy Garlic Parmesan Zoodles

Ingredients:

- 4 medium-sized zucchini, spiralized into noodles
- 2 tablespoons olive oil
- 4 cloves garlic, minced
- 1 cup heavy cream
- 1 cup grated Parmesan cheese
- Salt and black pepper to taste
- Crushed red pepper flakes (optional, for heat)
- Fresh parsley, chopped, for garnish

Instructions:

Prepare the Zoodles:
- Use a spiralizer to turn the zucchini into noodles. If you don't have a spiralizer, you can use a vegetable peeler to make ribbon-like strips.

Sauté Zoodles:
- Heat olive oil in a large skillet over medium heat. Add the spiralized zucchini noodles and sauté for 2-3 minutes until they are just tender but not mushy. Drain any excess water released by the zucchini.

Make the Creamy Garlic Parmesan Sauce:
- In the same skillet, add minced garlic and sauté for about 1-2 minutes until fragrant.
- Pour in the heavy cream, stirring continuously.
- Gradually add the grated Parmesan cheese while stirring to melt and incorporate it into the sauce.
- Season with salt, black pepper, and crushed red pepper flakes (if using). Adjust the seasonings to your taste.

Combine Zoodles and Sauce:
- Add the sautéed zucchini noodles back into the skillet, tossing them in the creamy garlic Parmesan sauce until well-coated.

Serve:
- Transfer the Creamy Garlic Parmesan Zoodles to a serving dish.
- Garnish with fresh chopped parsley and additional Parmesan cheese if desired.

Enjoy:
- Serve immediately, and enjoy your low-carb and flavorful meal!

This dish is quick to prepare and offers a healthier alternative to traditional pasta. It's a great way to incorporate more vegetables into your diet while still enjoying a creamy and satisfying dish.

Pesto Zoodles with Cherry Tomatoes

Ingredients:

For the Pesto:

    2 cups fresh basil leaves, packed
    1/2 cup grated Parmesan cheese
    1/2 cup pine nuts or walnuts
    3 cloves garlic, minced
    1/2 cup extra virgin olive oil
    Salt and black pepper to taste
    Juice of 1 lemon (optional)

For the Zoodles:

8. 4 medium-sized zucchini, spiralized into noodles

    1 tablespoon olive oil
    1 pint cherry tomatoes, halved
    Salt and black pepper to taste
    Grated Parmesan cheese for garnish
    Fresh basil leaves, chopped, for garnish

Instructions:

Prepare the Pesto:

    In a food processor, combine fresh basil, grated Parmesan cheese, pine nuts or walnuts, and minced garlic.
    Pulse the ingredients while slowly drizzling in the olive oil until the pesto reaches your desired consistency.
    Season with salt and black pepper to taste. If you like a bit of citrus flavor, you can add the juice of one lemon and pulse to combine.

Cook the Zoodles:

4. Heat olive oil in a large skillet over medium heat.

>Add the spiralized zucchini noodles to the skillet and sauté for 2-3 minutes until they are just tender. Drain any excess water released by the zucchini.
>Add the halved cherry tomatoes to the skillet with the zoodles and toss for an additional 1-2 minutes until the tomatoes are slightly softened.
>Season with salt and black pepper to taste.

Combine Pesto and Zoodles:

8. Add the prepared pesto to the skillet with the zoodles and cherry tomatoes. Toss everything together until the zoodles are evenly coated in the pesto.

>Adjust the seasoning if needed.

Serve:

10. Transfer the Pesto Zoodles with Cherry Tomatoes to a serving dish.

>Garnish with grated Parmesan cheese and chopped fresh basil.
>Serve immediately, and enjoy your flavorful and vibrant Pesto Zoodles with Cherry Tomatoes!

This dish is not only tasty but also a great way to incorporate more vegetables into your diet. It's perfect for a light and refreshing meal, especially during the warmer months.

One-Pan Chicken Alfredo

Ingredients:

>1 pound (about 450g) boneless, skinless chicken breasts, cut into bite-sized pieces
>Salt and black pepper to taste
>2 tablespoons olive oil
>3 cloves garlic, minced
>8 ounces (about 225g) fettuccine pasta

2 1/2 cups chicken broth
1 cup heavy cream
1 cup grated Parmesan cheese
1/2 cup unsalted butter
Fresh parsley, chopped, for garnish (optional)

Instructions:

Season and Cook Chicken:
- Season the bite-sized chicken pieces with salt and black pepper.
- Heat olive oil in a large skillet over medium-high heat.
- Add the seasoned chicken to the skillet and cook until browned on all sides and fully cooked through. Remove the cooked chicken from the skillet and set it aside.

Sauté Garlic and Toast Pasta:
- In the same skillet, add minced garlic and sauté for about 1 minute until fragrant.
- Break the fettuccine pasta into smaller pieces and add it to the skillet. Toast the pasta for 1-2 minutes until it starts to turn golden.

Add Broth and Cream:
- Pour in the chicken broth, heavy cream, and add the unsalted butter to the skillet with the toasted pasta. Stir to combine.

Cook Pasta:
- Bring the liquid to a simmer and reduce the heat to medium-low.
- Simmer the pasta in the broth mixture, stirring occasionally, until the pasta is cooked and the liquid has reduced to a creamy consistency. This may take about 10-12 minutes.

Finish with Parmesan and Chicken:
- Stir in the grated Parmesan cheese until it melts into the sauce.
- Add the cooked chicken back to the skillet, tossing everything together.

Garnish and Serve:
- Garnish with chopped fresh parsley if desired.
- Serve the One-Pan Chicken Alfredo immediately, and enjoy your creamy and comforting meal!

This recipe simplifies the classic Alfredo preparation by incorporating all the elements into one pan, making it a convenient option for a delicious weeknight dinner.

Lemon Garlic Shrimp Pasta

Ingredients:

8 ounces (about 225g) linguine or your favorite pasta
1 pound (about 450g) large shrimp, peeled and deveined
Salt and black pepper to taste
3 tablespoons olive oil
4 cloves garlic, minced
Zest of 1 lemon
Juice of 1 lemon
1/2 teaspoon red pepper flakes (optional, for heat)
1/2 cup chicken broth or white wine
1/4 cup chopped fresh parsley
Grated Parmesan cheese for serving (optional)

Instructions:

Cook the Pasta:
- Cook the linguine or pasta according to the package instructions in a large pot of salted boiling water until al dente. Reserve about 1/2 cup of pasta cooking water before draining.

Season and Cook Shrimp:
- Season the shrimp with salt and black pepper.
- In a large skillet, heat 2 tablespoons of olive oil over medium-high heat. Add the shrimp to the skillet and cook for 2-3 minutes per side or until they turn pink and opaque. Remove the shrimp from the skillet and set them aside.

Sauté Garlic and Lemon Zest:
- In the same skillet, add the remaining 1 tablespoon of olive oil.
- Add minced garlic and lemon zest to the skillet, sautéing for about 1-2 minutes until fragrant.

Deglaze with Broth or Wine:
- Pour in the chicken broth or white wine, scraping the bottom of the skillet to release any flavorful bits.

Add Lemon Juice and Red Pepper Flakes:
- Stir in the lemon juice and red pepper flakes (if using). Adjust the heat level to your preference.

Combine Shrimp and Pasta:

- Add the cooked shrimp back to the skillet, tossing them in the lemon garlic sauce.
- Add the cooked and drained pasta to the skillet, tossing everything together. If needed, add a bit of the reserved pasta cooking water to reach your desired consistency.

Finish and Garnish:
- Stir in chopped fresh parsley.
- Optionally, top with grated Parmesan cheese before serving.

Serve:
- Serve the Lemon Garlic Shrimp Pasta immediately, and enjoy your vibrant and flavorful dish!

This recipe is quick to make and perfect for a light and refreshing meal. The combination of citrusy lemon, garlic, and tender shrimp makes for a delightful pasta experience.

Pasta Primavera

Ingredients:

    8 ounces (about 225g) fettuccine or your favorite pasta
    2 tablespoons olive oil
    3 cloves garlic, minced
    1 medium-sized zucchini, julienned or sliced
    1 medium-sized yellow squash, julienned or sliced
    1 medium-sized carrot, julienned or sliced
    1 bell pepper (any color), thinly sliced
    1 cup cherry tomatoes, halved
    1 cup broccoli florets
    Salt and black pepper to taste
    1/2 teaspoon red pepper flakes (optional, for heat)
    1/4 cup fresh basil leaves, chopped
    1/4 cup fresh parsley, chopped
    Grated Parmesan cheese for serving (optional)

Instructions:

Cook the Pasta:
- Cook the fettuccine or pasta according to the package instructions in a large pot of salted boiling water until al dente. Reserve about 1/2 cup of pasta cooking water before draining.

Prepare the Vegetables:
- While the pasta is cooking, heat olive oil in a large skillet over medium heat.
- Add minced garlic and sauté for about 1 minute until fragrant.
- Add the julienned or sliced zucchini, yellow squash, carrot, bell pepper, cherry tomatoes, and broccoli to the skillet. Sauté the vegetables for 5-7 minutes or until they are tender-crisp.

Season the Vegetables:
- Season the vegetables with salt, black pepper, and red pepper flakes (if using). Adjust the seasoning to your taste.

Combine Pasta and Vegetables:
- Add the cooked and drained pasta to the skillet with the sautéed vegetables.

- Toss everything together, adding a bit of the reserved pasta cooking water if needed to reach your desired consistency.

Finish and Garnish:
- Stir in chopped fresh basil and parsley.
- Optionally, top with grated Parmesan cheese before serving.

Serve:
- Serve the Pasta Primavera immediately, and enjoy your colorful and vibrant dish!

Feel free to customize the vegetables based on what's in season or your personal preferences. This versatile and light pasta dish is perfect for showcasing the flavors of fresh, seasonal vegetables.

Seafood:
Lemon Herb Shrimp Skewers

Ingredients:

For the Marinade:

    1/4 cup olive oil
    3 tablespoons fresh lemon juice
    2 cloves garlic, minced
    1 teaspoon fresh thyme leaves (or 1/2 teaspoon dried thyme)
    1 teaspoon fresh rosemary leaves (or 1/2 teaspoon dried rosemary)
    1 teaspoon fresh parsley, chopped
    1 teaspoon Dijon mustard
    Salt and black pepper to taste

For the Shrimp Skewers:

9. 1 pound (about 450g) large shrimp, peeled and deveined

    Wooden or metal skewers

Instructions:

    Prepare the Marinade:
- In a bowl, whisk together olive oil, fresh lemon juice, minced garlic, fresh thyme leaves, fresh rosemary leaves, chopped parsley, Dijon mustard, salt, and black pepper.

    Marinate the Shrimp:
- Place the peeled and deveined shrimp in a shallow dish or a resealable plastic bag.
- Pour the marinade over the shrimp, ensuring they are well-coated. Marinate for at least 15-30 minutes, allowing the flavors to infuse.

    Preheat the Grill or Grill Pan:
- If using an outdoor grill, preheat it to medium-high heat. If using a grill pan indoors, heat it over medium-high heat on the stovetop.

    Skewer the Shrimp:
- Thread the marinated shrimp onto skewers, ensuring they are evenly distributed.

Grill the Shrimp Skewers:
- Place the shrimp skewers on the preheated grill or grill pan.
- Grill for approximately 2-3 minutes per side or until the shrimp are opaque and cooked through. Be careful not to overcook, as shrimp can become tough.

Serve:
- Once the shrimp skewers are cooked, remove them from the grill.
- Serve the Lemon Herb Shrimp Skewers immediately, and enjoy your flavorful and aromatic dish.

These Lemon Herb Shrimp Skewers are perfect for a light and refreshing meal, and they pair well with a variety of side dishes, such as rice, quinoa, or a fresh salad. The combination of zesty lemon and aromatic herbs adds a burst of flavor to the succulent shrimp.

Salmon and Asparagus Foil Packets

Ingredients:

    4 salmon fillets
    1 bunch of asparagus, trimmed
    2 tablespoons olive oil
    4 cloves garlic, minced
    1 lemon, sliced
    Salt and black pepper to taste
    Fresh herbs (such as dill, parsley, or thyme), chopped
    Optional: Red pepper flakes for a bit of heat

Instructions:

Preheat the Oven:
- Preheat your oven to 400°F (200°C).

Prepare Foil Packets:
- Cut four large pieces of aluminum foil.
- Place a salmon fillet in the center of each piece of foil.
- Arrange a handful of trimmed asparagus around each salmon fillet.

Season:
- Drizzle olive oil over each salmon fillet and asparagus bundle.
- Sprinkle minced garlic over the salmon and asparagus.
- Season with salt and black pepper to taste.
- Optionally, add red pepper flakes for a bit of heat.
- Top each salmon fillet with slices of lemon.

Seal Foil Packets:
- Fold the sides of the foil over the salmon and asparagus to create a packet, sealing the edges tightly.
- Place the foil packets on a baking sheet.

Bake:
- Bake in the preheated oven for about 15-20 minutes, or until the salmon is cooked through and flakes easily with a fork.

Garnish:
- Carefully open the foil packets.
- Sprinkle fresh herbs over the salmon and asparagus.

Serve:

- Serve the Salmon and Asparagus Foil Packets directly in the foil or transfer to plates.
- Enjoy your flavorful and healthy meal!

This recipe is not only easy to make but also preserves the natural flavors of the salmon and asparagus. The foil packets help the ingredients cook in their juices, resulting in a moist and delicious dish. Feel free to customize the recipe with your favorite herbs and seasonings.

Garlic Lemon Shrimp

Ingredients:

1 pound (about 450g) large shrimp, peeled and deveined
3 tablespoons olive oil
4 cloves garlic, minced
Zest of 1 lemon
Juice of 1 lemon
Salt and black pepper to taste
Red pepper flakes (optional, for heat)
Fresh parsley, chopped, for garnish

Instructions:

Prepare the Shrimp:
- Pat the peeled and deveined shrimp dry with paper towels.

Season the Shrimp:
- In a bowl, combine the shrimp with olive oil, minced garlic, lemon zest, lemon juice, salt, black pepper, and red pepper flakes (if using). Toss to coat the shrimp evenly.

Marinate:
- Allow the shrimp to marinate for about 15-30 minutes, allowing the flavors to meld.

Cook the Shrimp:
- Heat a large skillet or pan over medium-high heat.
- Add the marinated shrimp to the hot pan, spreading them out in a single layer.
- Cook the shrimp for 2-3 minutes on each side or until they are opaque and cooked through. Be careful not to overcook, as shrimp can become tough.

Garnish:
- Sprinkle chopped fresh parsley over the cooked shrimp.

Serve:
- Serve the Garlic Lemon Shrimp immediately, either as an appetizer or as a main dish.
- Optionally, you can serve the shrimp over cooked pasta, rice, or a bed of greens.

Enjoy:

- Enjoy your Garlic Lemon Shrimp with the bright and zesty flavors of garlic and lemon!

This recipe is perfect for a quick and light meal, and the combination of garlic and lemon adds a burst of freshness to the shrimp. It's versatile and can be paired with various side dishes to suit your preferences.

Baked Cod with Herbs

Ingredients:

    4 cod fillets (about 6 ounces each)
    2 tablespoons olive oil
    2 tablespoons fresh lemon juice
    2 cloves garlic, minced
    1 teaspoon dried oregano
    1 teaspoon dried thyme
    1 teaspoon dried rosemary
    Salt and black pepper to taste
    Lemon slices for garnish
    Fresh parsley, chopped, for garnish

Instructions:

Preheat the Oven:
- Preheat your oven to 400°F (200°C).

Prepare the Cod:
- Pat the cod fillets dry with paper towels.

Make the Herb Mixture:
- In a small bowl, mix together olive oil, fresh lemon juice, minced garlic, dried oregano, dried thyme, dried rosemary, salt, and black pepper.

Coat the Cod:
- Place the cod fillets on a baking sheet lined with parchment paper or lightly greased.
- Brush the herb mixture over the top of each cod fillet, ensuring they are well-coated.

Bake:
- Bake in the preheated oven for 12-15 minutes or until the cod is opaque and flakes easily with a fork. The cooking time may vary depending on the thickness of the fillets.

Garnish:
- Garnish the baked cod with lemon slices and chopped fresh parsley.

Serve:
- Serve the Baked Cod with Herbs immediately, and enjoy your light and flavorful dish!

This recipe allows the natural flavors of the cod to shine while adding a fragrant blend of herbs for depth. It's a quick and fuss-free way to prepare a healthy and delicious meal. You can pair the baked cod with your favorite side dishes such as roasted vegetables, quinoa, or a fresh salad.

Salmon Salad with Avocado

Ingredients:

For the Salmon:

    4 salmon fillets
    2 tablespoons olive oil
    Salt and black pepper to taste
    Lemon wedges for serving

For the Salad:

5. 4 cups mixed salad greens (spinach, arugula, or your favorite greens)

    1 cucumber, sliced
    1 cup cherry tomatoes, halved
    1 red onion, thinly sliced
    2 avocados, sliced

For the Dressing:

10. 3 tablespoons olive oil

    2 tablespoons balsamic vinegar
    1 teaspoon Dijon mustard
    1 clove garlic, minced
    Salt and black pepper to taste

Instructions:

Prepare the Salmon:

    Preheat your oven to 400°F (200°C).
    Place the salmon fillets on a baking sheet lined with parchment paper.
    Drizzle olive oil over the salmon fillets and season with salt and black pepper.
    Bake in the preheated oven for 12-15 minutes or until the salmon is cooked through and flakes easily with a fork.
    Squeeze fresh lemon juice over the baked salmon fillets before serving.

Prepare the Salad:

6. In a large salad bowl, combine the mixed greens, sliced cucumber, cherry tomatoes, red onion, and avocado.

Make the Dressing:

7. In a small bowl, whisk together olive oil, balsamic vinegar, Dijon mustard, minced garlic, salt, and black pepper.

Assemble the Salmon Salad:

8. Place the baked salmon fillets on top of the salad.

> Drizzle the dressing over the salad and salmon.
> Toss everything gently to combine, ensuring the salad is well-coated with the dressing.

Serve:

11. Divide the Salmon Salad with Avocado among serving plates.

> Optionally, garnish with additional lemon wedges and a sprinkle of fresh herbs. Serve immediately and enjoy your nutritious and delicious Salmon Salad with Avocado!

This salad is not only satisfying but also packed with healthy fats and protein. It makes for a fantastic light lunch or dinner option, and the combination of flavors is sure to delight your taste buds.

Cajun Baked Tilapia

Ingredients:

4 tilapia fillets
2 tablespoons olive oil
1 tablespoon Cajun seasoning
1 teaspoon paprika
1 teaspoon garlic powder
1 teaspoon onion powder
1/2 teaspoon dried thyme
1/2 teaspoon dried oregano
Salt and black pepper to taste
Lemon wedges for serving
Chopped fresh parsley for garnish (optional)

Instructions:

Preheat the Oven:
- Preheat your oven to 400°F (200°C).

Prepare the Cajun Seasoning Mix:
- In a small bowl, combine Cajun seasoning, paprika, garlic powder, onion powder, dried thyme, dried oregano, salt, and black pepper. Mix well to create the Cajun seasoning blend.

Season the Tilapia:
- Place the tilapia fillets on a baking sheet lined with parchment paper or lightly greased.
- Drizzle olive oil over the tilapia fillets, ensuring they are well-coated.
- Sprinkle the Cajun seasoning mix evenly over each tilapia fillet, pressing it gently onto the surface.

Bake:
- Bake in the preheated oven for 12-15 minutes or until the tilapia is cooked through and easily flakes with a fork.

Serve:
- Squeeze fresh lemon juice over the baked Cajun Tilapia fillets before serving.
- Optionally, garnish with chopped fresh parsley for a burst of color and added freshness.

Serve:
- Serve the Cajun Baked Tilapia with lemon wedges on the side.
- Enjoy your flavorful and spicy Cajun Baked Tilapia!

This recipe is a great way to add a Cajun twist to tilapia, and it's a quick and tasty option for a weeknight dinner. Pair it with your favorite side dishes, such as rice, quinoa, or a fresh salad.

Vegetarian:
Chickpea and Spinach Curry

Ingredients:

    2 tablespoons oil (vegetable or olive oil)
    1 large onion, finely chopped
    3 cloves garlic, minced
    1 tablespoon fresh ginger, grated
    1 can (15 ounces) chickpeas, drained and rinsed
    1 can (14 ounces) diced tomatoes
    1 can (14 ounces) coconut milk
    1 teaspoon ground cumin
    1 teaspoon ground coriander
    1 teaspoon turmeric powder
    1 teaspoon garam masala
    1/2 teaspoon chili powder (adjust to taste)
    Salt and black pepper to taste
    4 cups fresh spinach leaves, washed and chopped
    Fresh cilantro, chopped, for garnish
    Cooked rice or naan bread for serving

Instructions:

Sauté Onions, Garlic, and Ginger:
- Heat oil in a large pan or pot over medium heat. Add finely chopped onions and sauté until they become translucent.
- Add minced garlic and grated ginger. Sauté for an additional 1-2 minutes until fragrant.

Add Spices:
- Add ground cumin, ground coriander, turmeric powder, garam masala, and chili powder to the sautéed onions, garlic, and ginger. Stir well to coat the spices.

Add Chickpeas and Tomatoes:
- Add the drained and rinsed chickpeas to the pan, stirring to combine with the spice mixture.
- Pour in the diced tomatoes (with their juices) and cook for a few minutes until the tomatoes start to break down.

Pour in Coconut Milk:

- Pour in the coconut milk, stirring to combine. Bring the mixture to a simmer.

Season and Cook:
- Season the curry with salt and black pepper to taste. Simmer for about 15-20 minutes, allowing the flavors to meld and the sauce to thicken.

Add Spinach:
- Add the chopped spinach to the curry. Stir until the spinach wilts and is evenly distributed.

Adjust Seasoning:
- Taste the curry and adjust the seasoning if necessary. You can add more salt, pepper, or spice according to your preference.

Serve:
- Serve the Chickpea and Spinach Curry over cooked rice or with naan bread.
- Garnish with fresh cilantro and enjoy your flavorful and wholesome curry!

This Chickpea and Spinach Curry is not only delicious but also packed with protein and nutrients. It's a great vegetarian or vegan option for a satisfying and wholesome meal.

Mushroom and Spinach Quiche

Ingredients:

For the Quiche Filling:

1 tablespoon olive oil
1 small onion, finely chopped
2 cups mushrooms, sliced
2 cups fresh spinach, chopped
4 large eggs
1 cup milk (whole or 2%)
Salt and black pepper to taste
1 cup shredded cheese (Gruyere, Swiss, cheddar, or your choice)
1 teaspoon Dijon mustard (optional)

For the Quiche Crust:

10. 1 pre-made pie crust or homemade pie crust

1 tablespoon butter (optional, for greasing the pan)

Instructions:

Prepare the Quiche Crust:

Preheat your oven according to the pie crust instructions or to 375°F (190°C).
If using a pre-made pie crust, follow the package instructions for pre-baking or prepping the crust. If using homemade pie crust, roll it out and place it in a greased pie dish.
Optionally, you can prick the bottom of the crust with a fork to prevent it from puffing up during baking.
Pre-bake the crust if required or follow the package instructions. Remove it from the oven and set aside.

Prepare the Quiche Filling:

5. In a skillet, heat olive oil over medium heat. Add chopped onions and sauté until they become translucent.

> Add sliced mushrooms to the skillet and cook until they release their moisture and become golden brown.
> Add chopped spinach to the skillet and cook until wilted. Remove excess moisture if needed.
> In a bowl, whisk together eggs, milk, salt, and black pepper. Optionally, add Dijon mustard for extra flavor.
> Spread the sautéed mushroom and spinach mixture evenly over the pre-baked pie crust.
> Pour the egg and milk mixture over the vegetables.
> Sprinkle shredded cheese on top.

Bake the Quiche:

12. Bake in the preheated oven for 30-35 minutes or until the quiche is set and the top is golden brown.

> Allow the quiche to cool for a few minutes before slicing.

Serve:

14. Slice and serve the Mushroom and Spinach Quiche warm. It can be enjoyed on its own or with a side salad.

> Garnish with fresh herbs if desired.

Enjoy your Mushroom and Spinach Quiche for a flavorful and satisfying meal!

Cauliflower Rice Stir-Fry

Ingredients:

For the Cauliflower Rice:

> 1 large head of cauliflower, washed and trimmed
> 2 tablespoons olive oil
> Salt and black pepper to taste

For the Stir-Fry:

4. 2 tablespoons sesame oil

> 3 cloves garlic, minced
> 1 tablespoon fresh ginger, grated
> 1 cup carrots, julienned
> 1 cup bell peppers, thinly sliced
> 1 cup broccoli florets
> 1 cup snap peas, trimmed
> 1 cup cooked protein (chicken, shrimp, tofu, etc.)
> 3 tablespoons soy sauce
> 1 tablespoon oyster sauce (optional)
> 1 teaspoon rice vinegar
> 1 teaspoon Sriracha sauce (optional, for heat)
> Green onions, chopped, for garnish
> Sesame seeds for garnish

Instructions:

Prepare Cauliflower Rice:

> Cut the cauliflower into florets.
> Place the cauliflower florets in a food processor and pulse until they resemble rice-sized grains.
> Heat olive oil in a large skillet or wok over medium heat.

Add the riced cauliflower to the skillet, season with salt and black pepper, and sauté for 5-7 minutes or until the cauliflower is tender but not mushy.
Remove the cauliflower rice from the skillet and set aside.

Prepare the Stir-Fry:

6. In the same skillet or wok, heat sesame oil over medium-high heat.

Add minced garlic and grated ginger, sautéing for about 1 minute until fragrant.
Add julienned carrots, sliced bell peppers, broccoli florets, and snap peas to the skillet. Stir-fry for 5-7 minutes until the vegetables are crisp-tender.
Add the cooked protein (chicken, shrimp, tofu, etc.) to the vegetables and stir to combine.
In a small bowl, mix soy sauce, oyster sauce (if using), rice vinegar, and Sriracha sauce. Pour the sauce over the stir-fry.
Add the cooked cauliflower rice back to the skillet and toss everything together until well combined.
Cook for an additional 2-3 minutes to heat through.

Serve:

13. Garnish the Cauliflower Rice Stir-Fry with chopped green onions and sesame seeds.

Serve hot and enjoy your flavorful and low-carb stir-fry!

This Cauliflower Rice Stir-Fry is a tasty and nutritious alternative to traditional stir-fried rice. Feel free to customize the vegetables and protein based on your preferences for a delicious and healthy meal.

Chickpea Salad

Ingredients:

For the Salad:

    2 cans (15 ounces each) chickpeas, drained and rinsed
    1 cucumber, diced
    1 bell pepper (any color), diced
    1 cup cherry tomatoes, halved
    1/2 red onion, finely chopped
    1/2 cup Kalamata olives, pitted and sliced
    1/2 cup feta cheese, crumbled (optional)
    Fresh parsley or cilantro, chopped, for garnish

For the Dressing:

9. 1/4 cup extra-virgin olive oil

    2 tablespoons red wine vinegar
    1 clove garlic, minced
    1 teaspoon Dijon mustard
    1 teaspoon honey or maple syrup
    Salt and black pepper to taste

Instructions:

Prepare the Chickpeas:

    Rinse and drain the canned chickpeas thoroughly.
    If desired, you can pat the chickpeas dry with a clean kitchen towel to remove excess moisture.

Make the Dressing:

3. In a small bowl, whisk together olive oil, red wine vinegar, minced garlic, Dijon mustard, honey or maple syrup, salt, and black pepper. Set aside.

Assemble the Chickpea Salad:

4. In a large salad bowl, combine the drained chickpeas, diced cucumber, diced bell pepper, halved cherry tomatoes, finely chopped red onion, sliced Kalamata olives, and crumbled feta cheese (if using).

> Pour the dressing over the salad and toss gently to combine, ensuring everything is well coated.

Chill and Serve:

6. Allow the Chickpea Salad to chill in the refrigerator for at least 30 minutes to allow the flavors to meld.

> Before serving, garnish with freshly chopped parsley or cilantro.
> Serve the Chickpea Salad as a refreshing side dish or a light and satisfying main course.

Feel free to customize this recipe by adding other ingredients such as avocado, roasted red peppers, or artichoke hearts. This Chickpea Salad is not only delicious but also packed with fiber and protein, making it a healthy and satisfying option for a quick meal or potluck contribution.

Sweet Potato and Black Bean Quesadilla

Ingredients:

    2 medium sweet potatoes, peeled and diced
    1 can (15 ounces) black beans, drained and rinsed
    1 teaspoon ground cumin
    1 teaspoon chili powder
    1/2 teaspoon smoked paprika
    Salt and black pepper to taste
    4 large whole wheat or corn tortillas
    1 cup shredded cheese (cheddar, Monterey Jack, or a Mexican blend)
    1 avocado, sliced
    Fresh cilantro, chopped, for garnish
    Greek yogurt or salsa for serving (optional)

Instructions:

Prepare the Sweet Potatoes:

    Steam or boil the diced sweet potatoes until they are tender. Drain any excess water.
    In a bowl, mash the sweet potatoes using a fork or potato masher.

Prepare the Black Beans:

3. In a separate bowl, combine the black beans, ground cumin, chili powder, smoked paprika, salt, and black pepper. Mix well to coat the beans with the spices.

Assemble the Quesadillas:

4. Place a tortilla on a flat surface.

    Spread a layer of mashed sweet potatoes onto half of the tortilla.
    Spoon the seasoned black beans over the sweet potatoes.
    Sprinkle shredded cheese over the beans.
    Fold the tortilla in half, creating a semi-circle.

Cook the Quesadillas:

9. Heat a large skillet or griddle over medium heat.

> Place the assembled quesadilla on the hot skillet and cook for 2-3 minutes on each side or until the tortilla is golden brown, and the cheese is melted.
> Repeat the process for the remaining tortillas.

Serve:

12. Once cooked, slice the quesadillas into wedges.

> Top with sliced avocado and chopped cilantro.
> Serve with Greek yogurt or salsa on the side if desired.
> Enjoy your flavorful Sweet Potato and Black Bean Quesadilla!

This recipe is not only delicious but also provides a satisfying and wholesome meal with the combination of sweet potatoes, black beans, and gooey melted cheese. Feel free to customize the toppings and add your favorite ingredients to make it your own.

Soup:
Tomato Basil Soup

Ingredients:

- 2 tablespoons olive oil
- 1 onion, chopped
- 2 cloves garlic, minced
- 2 cans (28 ounces each) whole tomatoes
- 1 can (14 ounces) diced tomatoes
- 1/4 cup tomato paste
- 4 cups vegetable or chicken broth
- 1 teaspoon sugar
- Salt and black pepper to taste
- 1/2 cup fresh basil leaves, chopped (plus extra for garnish)
- 1/2 cup heavy cream (optional, for a creamy version)
- Grated Parmesan cheese for garnish (optional)
- Croutons for serving (optional)

Instructions:

Prepare the Soup Base:

- In a large pot, heat olive oil over medium heat.
- Add chopped onions and sauté until they become translucent.
- Add minced garlic and continue to sauté for about 1 minute until fragrant.

Add Tomatoes:

4. Pour in the whole tomatoes, diced tomatoes, and tomato paste. Break up the whole tomatoes with a spoon.

Season and Simmer:

5. Add vegetable or chicken broth, sugar, salt, and black pepper. Stir well.

Bring the soup to a boil, then reduce the heat to low and let it simmer for about 15-20 minutes to allow the flavors to meld.

Blend the Soup:

7. Using an immersion blender or by transferring the soup to a blender in batches, blend the soup until smooth and creamy.

Add Basil and Cream:

8. Stir in chopped fresh basil.

>   If you prefer a creamy version, add the heavy cream and stir until well combined. Adjust the seasoning if necessary.

Serve:

10. Ladle the Tomato Basil Soup into bowls.

>   Garnish with additional chopped basil, grated Parmesan cheese, and croutons if desired.
>   Serve hot and enjoy your comforting Tomato Basil Soup!

This recipe is a classic, but feel free to customize it by adding your favorite herbs or spices. It pairs well with a crusty baguette or a grilled cheese sandwich for a satisfying meal.

Lentil Soup

Ingredients:

- 1 cup dried green or brown lentils, rinsed and drained
- 2 tablespoons olive oil
- 1 onion, chopped
- 2 carrots, diced
- 2 celery stalks, diced
- 3 cloves garlic, minced
- 1 teaspoon ground cumin
- 1 teaspoon ground coriander
- 1 teaspoon smoked paprika
- 1/2 teaspoon turmeric powder
- 1 bay leaf
- 6 cups vegetable or chicken broth
- 1 can (14 ounces) diced tomatoes
- Salt and black pepper to taste
- 2 cups chopped leafy greens (such as spinach or kale)
- Juice of 1 lemon
- Fresh parsley, chopped, for garnish
- Optional: Red pepper flakes for heat

Instructions:

Prepare Lentils:

Rinse the lentils under cold water and drain.

Sauté Vegetables:

2. In a large pot, heat olive oil over medium heat.

Add chopped onions, carrots, and celery. Sauté until the vegetables are softened, about 5-7 minutes.
Add minced garlic and sauté for an additional 1-2 minutes until fragrant.

Add Spices:

5. Stir in ground cumin, ground coriander, smoked paprika, turmeric powder, and the bay leaf. Cook for 1-2 minutes to toast the spices.

Simmer Soup:

6. Pour in the vegetable or chicken broth and add the rinsed lentils.

> Add the diced tomatoes (with their juices) to the pot.
> Season with salt and black pepper to taste. Optionally, add red pepper flakes for heat.
> Bring the soup to a boil, then reduce the heat to low, cover, and simmer for about 25-30 minutes or until the lentils are tender.

Add Greens and Lemon Juice:

10. Stir in the chopped leafy greens and cook for an additional 3-5 minutes until the greens are wilted.

> Add the lemon juice and stir to combine.

Serve:

12. Remove the bay leaf from the soup.

> Ladle the Lentil Soup into bowls, garnish with chopped fresh parsley, and serve hot.

This Lentil Soup is not only delicious but also packed with protein and fiber. It's a versatile recipe, so feel free to customize it with your favorite herbs and spices. Enjoy it as a wholesome and comforting meal!

Butternut Squash Soup

Ingredients:

- 1 large butternut squash, peeled, seeded, and diced (about 4 cups)
- 1 onion, chopped
- 2 carrots, peeled and chopped
- 2 apples, peeled, cored, and chopped
- 3 cloves garlic, minced
- 2 tablespoons olive oil
- 4 cups vegetable or chicken broth
- 1 teaspoon ground cinnamon
- 1/2 teaspoon ground nutmeg
- Salt and black pepper to taste
- 1 cup coconut milk or heavy cream
- Optional toppings: toasted pumpkin seeds, croutons, or a drizzle of olive oil

Instructions:

Preheat the Oven:

Preheat your oven to 400°F (200°C).

Roast the Vegetables:

2. In a large bowl, toss the diced butternut squash, chopped onion, carrots, apples, and minced garlic with olive oil until evenly coated.

Spread the vegetables on a baking sheet in a single layer.
Roast in the preheated oven for about 30-40 minutes or until the vegetables are tender and slightly caramelized.

Blend the Soup:

5. Once the roasted vegetables are done, transfer them to a blender or use an immersion blender.

Add a portion of the broth and blend until smooth. Continue adding the remaining broth until you reach your desired consistency.

Cook on the Stove:

7. Pour the blended soup into a large pot.

Season the soup with ground cinnamon, ground nutmeg, salt, and black pepper. Stir well.
Place the pot over medium heat and bring the soup to a simmer. Allow it to cook for an additional 10-15 minutes to let the flavors meld.

Add Coconut Milk or Cream:

10. Stir in coconut milk or heavy cream, adjusting the thickness of the soup as desired.

Adjust Seasoning and Serve:

11. Taste the soup and adjust the seasoning if necessary.

Ladle the Butternut Squash Soup into bowls.

Garnish and Serve:

13. Garnish with your choice of toppings, such as toasted pumpkin seeds, croutons, or a drizzle of olive oil.

Serve the Butternut Squash Soup hot and enjoy this comforting and flavorful dish!

This recipe yields a creamy and velvety soup with the natural sweetness of butternut squash and a hint of warmth from the spices. It's perfect for a cozy meal during the fall and winter seasons.

Quick Minestrone Soup

Ingredients:

    2 tablespoons olive oil
    1 onion, chopped
    2 carrots, diced
    2 celery stalks, diced
    3 cloves garlic, minced
    1 can (14 ounces) diced tomatoes
    1 can (15 ounces) kidney beans, drained and rinsed
    4 cups vegetable broth
    1 teaspoon dried oregano
    1 teaspoon dried basil
    1/2 teaspoon dried thyme
    1 cup small pasta (e.g., ditalini or small shells)
    1 zucchini, diced
    1 cup green beans, trimmed and chopped
    1 cup chopped spinach or kale
    Salt and black pepper to taste
    Grated Parmesan cheese for serving (optional)
    Fresh basil or parsley, chopped, for garnish (optional)

Instructions:

Sauté Vegetables:

    In a large pot, heat olive oil over medium heat.
    Add chopped onions, diced carrots, diced celery, and minced garlic. Sauté until the vegetables are softened, about 5-7 minutes.

Add Tomatoes and Beans:

3. Add the diced tomatoes (with their juices) and kidney beans to the pot. Stir to combine.

Pour in Broth and Season:

4. Pour in the vegetable broth and add dried oregano, dried basil, dried thyme, salt, and black pepper. Stir well.

Bring to a Boil:

5. Increase the heat to bring the soup to a boil.

> Once boiling, add the small pasta to the pot and cook according to the package instructions until al dente.

Add Zucchini, Green Beans, and Greens:

7. Add diced zucchini, chopped green beans, and chopped spinach or kale to the pot. Cook for an additional 5-7 minutes until the vegetables are tender.

Adjust Seasoning:

8. Taste the soup and adjust the seasoning if necessary. Add more salt and pepper to suit your taste.

Serve:

9. Ladle the Quick Minestrone Soup into bowls.

> Optionally, garnish with grated Parmesan cheese and chopped fresh basil or parsley.
> Serve hot and enjoy your quick and delicious Minestrone Soup!

This quick version of Minestrone Soup is a wholesome and satisfying meal that's perfect for a busy day. Feel free to customize the vegetables and adjust the seasonings to your liking.

Tomato Basil Quinoa Soup

Ingredients:

    1 cup quinoa, rinsed and drained
    2 tablespoons olive oil
    1 onion, chopped
    2 carrots, diced
    2 celery stalks, diced
    3 cloves garlic, minced
    1 can (28 ounces) crushed tomatoes
    4 cups vegetable or chicken broth
    1 teaspoon dried basil
    1 teaspoon dried oregano
    Salt and black pepper to taste
    1/2 cup fresh basil leaves, chopped
    Grated Parmesan cheese for serving (optional)

Instructions:

Cook Quinoa:

    In a separate pot, cook the quinoa according to package instructions. Once cooked, set aside.

Sauté Vegetables:

2. In a large pot, heat olive oil over medium heat.

    Add chopped onions, diced carrots, diced celery, and minced garlic. Sauté until the vegetables are softened, about 5-7 minutes.

Add Tomatoes and Broth:

4. Pour in the crushed tomatoes and vegetable or chicken broth. Stir well.

    Add dried basil, dried oregano, salt, and black pepper. Mix to combine.

Simmer:

6. Bring the soup to a boil, then reduce the heat to low and let it simmer for about 15-20 minutes, allowing the flavors to meld.

Add Cooked Quinoa and Fresh Basil:

7. Add the cooked quinoa to the pot.

> Stir in the chopped fresh basil.

Adjust Seasoning:

9. Taste the soup and adjust the seasoning if necessary. Add more salt and pepper to suit your taste.

Serve:

10. Ladle the Tomato Basil Quinoa Soup into bowls.

> Optionally, garnish with grated Parmesan cheese.
> Serve hot and enjoy your nutritious and flavorful Tomato Basil Quinoa Soup!

This soup is not only tasty but also packed with protein and fiber from the quinoa. It's a wholesome option for a comforting and satisfying meal.

Coconut Curry Lentil Soup

Ingredients:

    1 cup dried lentils (red or green), rinsed and drained
    1 tablespoon coconut oil or olive oil
    1 onion, chopped
    3 cloves garlic, minced
    1 tablespoon fresh ginger, grated
    1 tablespoon curry powder
    1 teaspoon ground cumin
    1 teaspoon ground turmeric
    1 can (14 ounces) diced tomatoes
    1 can (14 ounces) coconut milk
    4 cups vegetable broth
    Salt and black pepper to taste
    Juice of 1 lime
    Fresh cilantro, chopped, for garnish
    Cooked rice for serving (optional)

Instructions:

Sauté Aromatics:

    In a large pot, heat coconut oil or olive oil over medium heat.
    Add chopped onions, minced garlic, and grated ginger. Sauté until the onions are softened.

Add Spices:

3. Stir in curry powder, ground cumin, and ground turmeric. Cook for an additional 1-2 minutes until the spices are fragrant.

Add Lentils and Tomatoes:

4. Add rinsed lentils to the pot and stir to coat them with the spices.

    Pour in the diced tomatoes (with their juices) and stir to combine.

Pour in Coconut Milk and Broth:

6. Pour in the coconut milk and vegetable broth. Stir well.

   Season with salt and black pepper to taste.

Simmer:

8. Bring the soup to a boil, then reduce the heat to low, cover, and simmer for about 20-25 minutes or until the lentils are tender.

Finish and Serve:

9. Stir in the lime juice to add a burst of freshness.

   Taste the soup and adjust the seasoning if necessary.
   Serve the Coconut Curry Lentil Soup hot, garnished with fresh cilantro.
   Optionally, serve over cooked rice for a more substantial meal.

Enjoy your delicious and aromatic Coconut Curry Lentil Soup! It's a perfect combination of spices, lentils, and coconut milk for a comforting and satisfying bowl of soup.

Salad:
Greek Salad

Ingredients:

For the Salad:

    1 cucumber, diced
    1 bell pepper (any color), diced
    1 pint cherry tomatoes, halved
    1 red onion, thinly sliced
    1 cup Kalamata olives, pitted
    1 cup feta cheese, crumbled
    1/2 cup fresh parsley, chopped

For the Dressing:

8. 1/4 cup extra-virgin olive oil

    2 tablespoons red wine vinegar
    1 teaspoon dried oregano
    1 teaspoon Dijon mustard
    Salt and black pepper to taste

Instructions:

Prepare the Vegetables:

    In a large salad bowl, combine diced cucumber, diced bell pepper, halved cherry tomatoes, thinly sliced red onion, Kalamata olives, and crumbled feta cheese. Add chopped fresh parsley to the bowl.

Make the Dressing:

3. In a small bowl, whisk together extra-virgin olive oil, red wine vinegar, dried oregano, Dijon mustard, salt, and black pepper.

    Adjust the seasoning to taste.

Toss and Serve:

5. Pour the dressing over the salad.

> Gently toss the salad to ensure all ingredients are well coated with the dressing. Allow the salad to marinate for a few minutes before serving to let the flavors meld.

Serve:

8. Serve the Greek Salad in individual bowls or on a platter.

> Optionally, garnish with additional fresh parsley or extra crumbled feta cheese. Enjoy your delicious and vibrant Greek Salad!

This classic Greek Salad is perfect as a refreshing side dish or a light meal on its own. It's versatile, and you can customize it by adding ingredients like cherry tomatoes, cucumbers, or red onions based on your preferences.

Cucumber and Tomato Salad

Ingredients:

    3 large tomatoes, diced
    2 cucumbers, sliced
    1/2 red onion, thinly sliced
    1/4 cup fresh basil or parsley, chopped
    2 tablespoons extra-virgin olive oil
    1 tablespoon red wine vinegar or balsamic vinegar
    Salt and black pepper to taste
    Feta cheese, crumbled (optional)

Instructions:

Prepare the Vegetables:

    In a large salad bowl, combine diced tomatoes, sliced cucumbers, thinly sliced red onion, and chopped fresh basil or parsley.

Make the Dressing:

2. In a small bowl, whisk together extra-virgin olive oil, red wine vinegar or balsamic vinegar, salt, and black pepper.

    Adjust the seasoning to taste.

Toss and Serve:

4. Pour the dressing over the vegetables.

    Gently toss the salad to ensure all ingredients are well coated with the dressing. Allow the salad to marinate for a few minutes before serving to let the flavors meld.

Optional: Add Feta Cheese:

7. If desired, crumble feta cheese over the salad just before serving. The creamy and salty flavor of feta complements the freshness of the vegetables.

Serve:

8. Serve the Cucumber and Tomato Salad in individual bowls or on a platter.

> Optionally, garnish with additional fresh basil or parsley.
> Enjoy your light and flavorful Cucumber and Tomato Salad!

This salad is perfect for a quick and healthy side dish or a light lunch. It's versatile and can be customized by adding ingredients like olives, red or yellow bell peppers, or avocado. Feel free to adjust the dressing to suit your taste preferences.

Cobb Salad

Ingredients:

For the Salad:

- 4 cups mixed salad greens (e.g., romaine lettuce, iceberg lettuce)
- 2 cups cooked and chopped chicken breast
- 4 hard-boiled eggs, sliced
- 1 cup cherry tomatoes, halved
- 1 avocado, diced
- 1/2 cup crumbled blue cheese or feta cheese
- 1/2 cup cooked and crumbled bacon
- 1/2 cup thinly sliced red onion
- 1 cup cucumber, diced (optional)
- 1 cup corn kernels, cooked (optional)

For the Dressing:

11. 1/4 cup extra-virgin olive oil

- 2 tablespoons red wine vinegar
- 1 teaspoon Dijon mustard
- 1 clove garlic, minced
- Salt and black pepper to taste

Instructions:

Prepare the Salad:

In a large salad bowl or on a platter, arrange the mixed salad greens. Arrange the chopped chicken, hard-boiled eggs, cherry tomatoes, diced avocado, crumbled blue cheese or feta, crumbled bacon, sliced red onion, cucumber (if using), and corn kernels (if using) over the salad greens in rows or sections.

Make the Dressing:

3. In a small bowl, whisk together extra-virgin olive oil, red wine vinegar, Dijon mustard, minced garlic, salt, and black pepper.

Adjust the seasoning to taste.

Serve:

5. Drizzle the dressing over the Cobb Salad just before serving.

Optionally, toss the salad gently to coat the ingredients with the dressing.
Serve immediately, and enjoy your delicious and satisfying Cobb Salad!

Cobb Salad is versatile, and you can customize it based on your preferences. Feel free to add or omit ingredients to suit your taste. This salad makes for a hearty meal on its own or a substantial side dish for lunch or dinner.

Spinach and Strawberry Salad

Ingredients:

For the Salad:

- 6 cups fresh baby spinach leaves, washed and dried
- 2 cups strawberries, hulled and sliced
- 1/2 cup red onion, thinly sliced
- 1/2 cup feta cheese, crumbled
- 1/2 cup candied pecans or walnuts, chopped (optional)
- 1/4 cup fresh basil leaves, torn

For the Dressing:

7. 3 tablespoons extra-virgin olive oil

- 2 tablespoons balsamic vinegar
- 1 tablespoon honey or maple syrup
- 1 teaspoon Dijon mustard
- Salt and black pepper to taste

Instructions:

Prepare the Salad:

In a large salad bowl, place the fresh baby spinach leaves.
Top the spinach with sliced strawberries, thinly sliced red onion, crumbled feta cheese, candied pecans or walnuts (if using), and torn fresh basil leaves.

Make the Dressing:

3. In a small bowl, whisk together extra-virgin olive oil, balsamic vinegar, honey or maple syrup, Dijon mustard, salt, and black pepper.

Adjust the seasoning to taste.

Serve:

5. Drizzle the dressing over the Spinach and Strawberry Salad just before serving.

> Toss the salad gently to coat the ingredients with the dressing.
> Serve immediately, and enjoy this light and flavorful Spinach and Strawberry Salad!

Feel free to customize the salad by adding grilled chicken or avocado for extra protein, or adjusting the sweetness of the dressing according to your preference. This salad is perfect for a refreshing and nutritious side dish or a light and satisfying main course.

Avocado and Chickpea Salad

Ingredients:

For the Salad:

- 2 cans (15 ounces each) chickpeas, drained and rinsed
- 2 avocados, diced
- 1 cup cherry tomatoes, halved
- 1/2 red onion, finely chopped
- 1/4 cup fresh cilantro or parsley, chopped
- 1/4 cup feta cheese, crumbled (optional)
- Salt and black pepper to taste

For the Dressing:

8. 3 tablespoons extra-virgin olive oil

- 1 tablespoon balsamic vinegar
- 1 teaspoon Dijon mustard
- 1 clove garlic, minced
- Juice of 1 lime
- Salt and black pepper to taste

Instructions:

Prepare the Salad:

In a large salad bowl, combine the drained and rinsed chickpeas, diced avocados, halved cherry tomatoes, finely chopped red onion, chopped cilantro or parsley, and crumbled feta cheese (if using).
Season the salad with salt and black pepper to taste.

Make the Dressing:

3. In a small bowl, whisk together extra-virgin olive oil, balsamic vinegar, Dijon mustard, minced garlic, lime juice, salt, and black pepper.

Adjust the seasoning to taste.

Serve:

5. Drizzle the dressing over the Avocado and Chickpea Salad just before serving.

   Gently toss the salad to coat the ingredients with the dressing.
   Serve immediately, and enjoy this nutritious and flavorful Avocado and Chickpea Salad!

This salad is not only quick to prepare but also provides a satisfying combination of creamy avocados, hearty chickpeas, and vibrant vegetables. It makes for a great side dish or a light and healthy main course. Feel free to customize it by adding additional vegetables or herbs based on your preferences.

Cucumber and Feta Salad

Ingredients:

    3 large cucumbers, thinly sliced
    1 cup cherry tomatoes, halved
    1/2 red onion, thinly sliced
    1/2 cup feta cheese, crumbled
    1/4 cup Kalamata olives, pitted and sliced
    2 tablespoons fresh dill, chopped (optional)
    2 tablespoons extra-virgin olive oil
    1 tablespoon red wine vinegar
    Salt and black pepper to taste

Instructions:

Prepare the Vegetables:

    In a large salad bowl, combine the thinly sliced cucumbers, halved cherry tomatoes, thinly sliced red onion, crumbled feta cheese, sliced Kalamata olives, and chopped fresh dill (if using).

Make the Dressing:

2. In a small bowl, whisk together extra-virgin olive oil, red wine vinegar, salt, and black pepper.

    Adjust the seasoning to taste.

Serve:

4. Drizzle the dressing over the Cucumber and Feta Salad just before serving.

    Gently toss the salad to coat the ingredients with the dressing.
    Serve immediately, and enjoy this light and flavorful Cucumber and Feta Salad!

This salad is perfect as a refreshing side dish for summer or a light lunch. The combination of crisp cucumbers, tangy feta cheese, and briny olives creates a delicious and satisfying salad. Feel free to customize it by adding additional herbs or ingredients like avocado if desired.

Side Dish:
Roasted Brussels Sprouts

Ingredients:

- 1 pound Brussels sprouts, trimmed and halved
- 2 tablespoons olive oil
- Salt and black pepper to taste
- Optional: Garlic powder, smoked paprika, or Parmesan cheese for extra flavor

Instructions:

Preheat the Oven:

Preheat your oven to 400°F (200°C).

Prepare Brussels Sprouts:

2. Trim the ends of the Brussels sprouts and cut them in half.

Remove any loose or yellow outer leaves.

Roast Brussels Sprouts:

4. Place the halved Brussels sprouts on a baking sheet.

Drizzle olive oil over the Brussels sprouts, ensuring they are well coated. Toss them to distribute the oil evenly.
Season with salt and black pepper. If desired, add garlic powder, smoked paprika, or any other seasonings of your choice for extra flavor.
Spread the Brussels sprouts in a single layer on the baking sheet.

Roast in the Oven:

8. Roast in the preheated oven for 20-25 minutes or until the Brussels sprouts are golden brown and crispy on the edges. Stir or shake the pan halfway through the cooking time for even roasting.

Serve:

9. Once roasted, remove the Brussels sprouts from the oven.

> Optionally, sprinkle Parmesan cheese over the roasted Brussels sprouts while they are still warm.
> Serve immediately and enjoy your delicious Roasted Brussels Sprouts!

Roasting Brussels sprouts enhances their natural flavors and brings out a delightful caramelization. Adjust the seasonings and add your favorite spices or herbs to personalize this simple and tasty side dish. It's a great accompaniment to various main courses.

Cauliflower Rice Stir-Fry

Ingredients:

For the Cauliflower Rice:

    1 large cauliflower head, washed and cut into florets
    2 tablespoons olive oil
    Salt and black pepper to taste

For the Stir-Fry:

4. 2 tablespoons sesame oil or vegetable oil

    1 onion, thinly sliced
    2 carrots, julienned
    1 bell pepper (any color), thinly sliced
    1 cup broccoli florets
    2 cloves garlic, minced
    1 tablespoon fresh ginger, grated
    1 cup snap peas, trimmed
    2 cups cooked protein of choice (tofu, chicken, shrimp, or beef)
    3 tablespoons low-sodium soy sauce or tamari
    1 tablespoon oyster sauce (optional)
    1 teaspoon rice vinegar
    Green onions, sliced, for garnish
    Sesame seeds, for garnish

Instructions:

Prepare Cauliflower Rice:

    In a food processor, pulse the cauliflower florets until they resemble rice-like grains.
    Heat olive oil in a large skillet over medium heat.
    Add the cauliflower rice to the skillet, season with salt and black pepper, and sauté for 5-7 minutes until tender. Set aside.

Prepare the Stir-Fry:

4. In the same skillet, heat sesame oil or vegetable oil over medium-high heat.

   Add sliced onions, julienned carrots, and bell pepper. Sauté for 3-5 minutes until the vegetables are slightly softened.
   Add broccoli florets, minced garlic, and grated ginger. Continue to sauté for an additional 2-3 minutes.
   Add snap peas and cooked protein (tofu, chicken, shrimp, or beef). Stir to combine.
   Pour in low-sodium soy sauce, oyster sauce (if using), and rice vinegar. Stir well to coat the ingredients.
   Add the prepared cauliflower rice to the stir-fry. Toss everything together until well combined and heated through.

Serve:

10. Garnish the Cauliflower Rice Stir-Fry with sliced green onions and sesame seeds.

    Taste and adjust the seasoning if necessary.
    Serve hot, and enjoy your flavorful and low-carb Cauliflower Rice Stir-Fry!

This recipe is versatile, and you can customize it by adding your favorite vegetables or adjusting the seasonings to suit your taste. It's a great option for a quick and healthy stir-fry with a low-carb twist.

Roasted Sweet Potato Wedges

Ingredients:

- 2 large sweet potatoes, washed and scrubbed
- 2 tablespoons olive oil
- 1 teaspoon paprika
- 1 teaspoon garlic powder
- 1 teaspoon onion powder
- 1/2 teaspoon cayenne pepper (adjust to taste)
- Salt and black pepper to taste
- Fresh parsley, chopped, for garnish (optional)

Instructions:

Preheat the Oven:

Preheat your oven to 425°F (220°C).

Prepare Sweet Potatoes:

2. Cut the sweet potatoes into wedges. You can leave the skin on for added texture and nutrients.

Coat with Seasonings:

3. In a large bowl, toss the sweet potato wedges with olive oil, paprika, garlic powder, onion powder, cayenne pepper, salt, and black pepper. Make sure the wedges are evenly coated with the seasonings.

Arrange on Baking Sheet:

4. Place the seasoned sweet potato wedges on a baking sheet in a single layer. Ensure they are not crowded to allow for even roasting.

Roast in the Oven:

5. Roast in the preheated oven for 25-30 minutes or until the sweet potatoes are tender and the edges are crispy. Flip the wedges halfway through the roasting time to ensure even cooking.

Serve:

6. Once roasted, remove the sweet potato wedges from the oven.

    Garnish with fresh chopped parsley if desired.
    Serve hot as a side dish or snack.

Enjoy your flavorful and healthy Roasted Sweet Potato Wedges! They make a delicious accompaniment to various meals or can be enjoyed on their own.

Quinoa and Black Bean Stuffed Bell Peppers

Ingredients:

For the Stuffed Bell Peppers:

    4 large bell peppers, halved and seeds removed
    1 cup quinoa, rinsed
    2 cups vegetable broth or water
    1 can (15 ounces) black beans, drained and rinsed
    1 cup corn kernels (fresh, frozen, or canned)
    1 cup diced tomatoes
    1 cup shredded cheese (cheddar, Monterey Jack, or your choice)
    1 teaspoon ground cumin
    1 teaspoon chili powder
    1/2 teaspoon garlic powder
    Salt and black pepper to taste
    Olive oil for drizzling

For Garnish:

13. Fresh cilantro, chopped

    Avocado slices
    Greek yogurt or sour cream

Instructions:

Prepare Quinoa:

    In a medium saucepan, combine quinoa and vegetable broth (or water). Bring to a boil, then reduce heat to low, cover, and simmer for about 15 minutes or until the quinoa is cooked and liquid is absorbed. Fluff with a fork.

Prepare Bell Peppers:

2. Preheat the oven to 375°F (190°C).

    Cut the bell peppers in half lengthwise and remove the seeds and membranes. Place the bell pepper halves in a baking dish.

Prepare Filling:

5. In a large bowl, combine cooked quinoa, black beans, corn, diced tomatoes, shredded cheese, ground cumin, chili powder, garlic powder, salt, and black pepper. Mix well.

Stuff the Bell Peppers:

6. Stuff each bell pepper half with the quinoa and black bean mixture, pressing down gently.

> Drizzle olive oil over the stuffed bell peppers.

Bake:

8. Cover the baking dish with aluminum foil.

> Bake in the preheated oven for 25-30 minutes or until the bell peppers are tender. Remove the foil and bake for an additional 5-10 minutes until the cheese is melted and bubbly.

Serve:

11. Remove from the oven and let the stuffed bell peppers cool slightly.

> Garnish with chopped cilantro and serve with avocado slices and a dollop of Greek yogurt or sour cream.

Enjoy your delicious and wholesome Quinoa and Black Bean Stuffed Bell Peppers! They make for a satisfying vegetarian meal or a flavorful side dish.

Parmesan Roasted Broccoli

Ingredients:

- 1 pound broccoli florets
- 2 tablespoons olive oil
- 1/2 cup grated Parmesan cheese
- 2 cloves garlic, minced
- 1 teaspoon lemon zest (optional)
- Salt and black pepper to taste
- Crushed red pepper flakes (optional, for a bit of heat)

Instructions:

Preheat the Oven:

Preheat your oven to 425°F (220°C).

Prepare Broccoli:

2. Wash and trim the broccoli into florets.

In a large bowl, toss the broccoli florets with olive oil until well coated.

Season and Roast:

4. Spread the broccoli in a single layer on a baking sheet.

Sprinkle grated Parmesan cheese, minced garlic, lemon zest (if using), salt, and black pepper over the broccoli.
Toss the broccoli to ensure even coating of the seasonings.

Roast in the Oven:

7. Roast in the preheated oven for 20-25 minutes or until the broccoli is tender and the edges are crispy.

If desired, sprinkle some crushed red pepper flakes over the roasted broccoli for a bit of heat.

Serve:

9. Once roasted, remove the Parmesan Roasted Broccoli from the oven.

   Transfer to a serving dish and serve hot.

Enjoy your Parmesan Roasted Broccoli as a tasty and nutritious side dish! The combination of roasted broccoli with Parmesan cheese adds a savory and satisfying flavor to this simple vegetable dish.

Sesame Soy Marinated Tofu

Ingredients:

For the Marinade:

    1 block (14-16 ounces) extra-firm tofu, pressed and cubed
    3 tablespoons soy sauce or tamari (for a gluten-free option)
    1 tablespoon sesame oil
    1 tablespoon rice vinegar
    1 tablespoon maple syrup or agave nectar
    2 cloves garlic, minced
    1 teaspoon grated fresh ginger
    1 tablespoon sesame seeds
    Green onions, chopped, for garnish (optional)

Instructions:

Prepare Tofu:

    Press the tofu to remove excess water. Cut the pressed tofu into cubes.

Prepare Marinade:

2. In a bowl, whisk together soy sauce or tamari, sesame oil, rice vinegar, maple syrup or agave nectar, minced garlic, grated ginger, and sesame seeds.

Marinate Tofu:

3. Place the tofu cubes in a shallow dish or a resealable plastic bag.

    Pour the marinade over the tofu, ensuring that the cubes are well coated. Allow the tofu to marinate for at least 30 minutes, or for a more intense flavor, marinate for a few hours or overnight in the refrigerator.

Cook Tofu:

6. Preheat the oven to 400°F (200°C).

    Place the marinated tofu cubes on a lined baking sheet in a single layer.

Bake for 25-30 minutes or until the tofu is golden brown and slightly crispy, flipping the cubes halfway through the baking time for even cooking.

Serve:

9. Once baked, remove the Sesame Soy Marinated Tofu from the oven.

> Garnish with chopped green onions if desired.
> Serve hot as a protein-packed main dish or as an addition to salads, stir-fries, or rice bowls.

Enjoy your Sesame Soy Marinated Tofu with its savory, sweet, and nutty flavors! It's a versatile dish that pairs well with a variety of sides and can be used in different culinary applications.

Dessert:
Chia Seed Pudding with Berries

Ingredients:

For the Chia Seed Pudding:

    1/4 cup chia seeds
    1 cup almond milk (or any milk of your choice)
    1-2 tablespoons maple syrup or honey (adjust to taste)
    1/2 teaspoon vanilla extract (optional)

For Topping:

5. Mixed berries (strawberries, blueberries, raspberries)

    Granola (optional)
    Honey or maple syrup for drizzling (optional)
    Mint leaves for garnish (optional)

Instructions:

Prepare Chia Seed Pudding:

    In a bowl, combine chia seeds, almond milk, maple syrup or honey, and vanilla extract (if using).
    Whisk the ingredients together until well combined.
    Let the mixture sit for a few minutes, then whisk again to prevent clumping.
    Cover the bowl and refrigerate for at least 2-3 hours or overnight, allowing the chia seeds to absorb the liquid and create a pudding-like consistency.

Assemble the Chia Seed Pudding with Berries:

5. Once the chia seed pudding has set, give it a good stir.

    Spoon the chia seed pudding into serving glasses or bowls.
    Top with a generous amount of mixed berries.
    Optionally, add a layer of granola for crunch.
    Drizzle honey or maple syrup over the top for extra sweetness, if desired.
    Garnish with mint leaves for a fresh touch.

Serve:

11. Serve the Chia Seed Pudding with Berries immediately or refrigerate until ready to serve.

>Enjoy this delightful and nutritious treat!

Chia Seed Pudding with Berries is not only delicious but also rich in fiber, omega-3 fatty acids, and antioxidants. It makes for a satisfying and healthy breakfast or a guilt-free dessert. Feel free to customize the toppings based on your preferences.

Fruit Salad with Mint

Ingredients:

- 2 cups watermelon, cubed
- 1 cup strawberries, hulled and halved
- 1 cup grapes, halved
- 1 cup pineapple, diced
- 1 cup blueberries
- 1 cup kiwi, peeled and sliced
- 2 tablespoons fresh mint leaves, chopped
- 1-2 tablespoons honey or maple syrup (optional, for added sweetness)
- Juice of 1 lime or lemon

Instructions:

Prepare the Fruits:

Wash and prepare all the fruits according to the specifications (cubed, halved, diced, sliced).

Assemble the Fruit Salad:

2. In a large bowl, combine watermelon, strawberries, grapes, pineapple, blueberries, and kiwi.

- Add the chopped mint leaves to the bowl.
- Drizzle honey or maple syrup over the fruit salad if you desire added sweetness.
- Squeeze the juice of one lime or lemon over the fruit salad for a citrusy kick.

Toss Gently:

6. Gently toss the fruit salad to combine all the ingredients.

Chill:

7. Cover the bowl and refrigerate the fruit salad for at least 30 minutes to let the flavors meld.

Serve:

8. Before serving, give the fruit salad a final gentle toss.

> Serve the Fruit Salad with Mint in individual bowls or as a refreshing side dish. Enjoy your vibrant and delicious fruit salad with the delightful addition of mint!

This Fruit Salad with Mint is not only a visually appealing dish but also a healthy and hydrating option. The mint adds a burst of freshness to the sweet and juicy fruits. Feel free to customize the fruit selection based on what's in season or your personal preferences.

Fruit Salsa with Cinnamon Chips

Ingredients:

For the Fruit Salsa:

    1 cup strawberries, diced
    1 cup kiwi, peeled and diced
    1 cup pineapple, diced
    1 cup mango, diced
    1/2 cup blueberries
    1 tablespoon fresh mint, chopped
    1 tablespoon honey or maple syrup (optional, for added sweetness)
    Juice of 1 lime

For the Cinnamon Chips:

9. 10 small flour tortillas

    2 tablespoons melted butter
    1/4 cup granulated sugar
    1 teaspoon ground cinnamon

Instructions:

Prepare the Fruit Salsa:

    In a bowl, combine diced strawberries, kiwi, pineapple, mango, blueberries, and chopped mint.
    Drizzle honey or maple syrup over the fruit salsa if you desire added sweetness.
    Squeeze the juice of one lime over the fruit salsa.
    Gently toss the fruit salsa to combine all the ingredients.
    Cover the bowl and refrigerate the fruit salsa for at least 30 minutes to let the flavors meld.

Prepare the Cinnamon Chips:

6. Preheat the oven to 350°F (175°C).

> Brush each tortilla with melted butter on both sides.
> In a small bowl, mix granulated sugar and ground cinnamon.
> Sprinkle the cinnamon-sugar mixture over each buttered tortilla, ensuring both sides are coated.
> Stack the tortillas and cut them into wedges using a pizza cutter.
> Arrange the cinnamon-coated tortilla wedges on a baking sheet in a single layer.
> Bake in the preheated oven for 10-12 minutes or until the chips are crispy and golden brown.

Serve:

13. Once the cinnamon chips are cooled, serve them alongside the chilled Fruit Salsa.

> Enjoy your delicious and festive Fruit Salsa with Cinnamon Chips!

This Fruit Salsa with Cinnamon Chips is a perfect dish for parties, picnics, or as a refreshing dessert. The combination of sweet and juicy fruits with the crispy and cinnamon-spiced chips is sure to be a hit. Feel free to customize the fruit selection based on what's in season or your personal preferences.

Chocolate Banana Smoothie

Ingredients:

2 ripe bananas, peeled and sliced
1 cup milk (dairy or plant-based)
1 tablespoon unsweetened cocoa powder
1-2 tablespoons honey or maple syrup (adjust to taste)
1/2 teaspoon vanilla extract
1 cup ice cubes
Optional toppings: whipped cream, chocolate shavings, banana slices

Instructions:

Prepare the Ingredients:
- Ensure the bananas are ripe for a sweeter flavor.
- Measure out the milk, cocoa powder, honey or maple syrup, and vanilla extract.

Blend the Ingredients:
- In a blender, combine the sliced bananas, milk, cocoa powder, honey or maple syrup, and vanilla extract.
- Add the ice cubes to the blender.

Blend Until Smooth:
- Blend all the ingredients until smooth and creamy.
- If the smoothie is too thick, you can add more milk to reach your desired consistency.

Taste and Adjust:
- Taste the smoothie and adjust the sweetness by adding more honey or maple syrup if needed.

Serve:
- Pour the Chocolate Banana Smoothie into glasses.

Optional Toppings:
- If desired, top the smoothie with whipped cream, chocolate shavings, or banana slices for an extra treat.

Enjoy:
- Serve the Chocolate Banana Smoothie immediately and enjoy your delicious and indulgent treat!

This Chocolate Banana Smoothie is not only tasty but also provides a good dose of potassium from the bananas and the satisfaction of chocolate flavor. It makes for a quick and delightful breakfast or a refreshing snack.

Apple Nachos

Ingredients:

- 2-3 large apples (such as Honeycrisp or Gala), cored and thinly sliced
- 1/4 cup smooth peanut butter or almond butter
- 1/4 cup chocolate chips
- 1/4 cup shredded coconut
- 1/4 cup chopped nuts (such as almonds, walnuts, or pecans)
- 1/4 cup dried cranberries or raisins
- 1 tablespoon honey or maple syrup (optional, for drizzling)
- 1 teaspoon ground cinnamon

Instructions:

Prepare the Apple Slices:

Core and thinly slice the apples. Arrange the apple slices in a single layer on a large serving platter.

Top with Peanut Butter:

2. Warm the peanut butter in the microwave for a few seconds until it becomes slightly more pourable.

Drizzle the warm peanut butter over the apple slices.

Add Toppings:

4. Sprinkle chocolate chips, shredded coconut, chopped nuts, and dried cranberries or raisins over the apple slices.

Drizzle with Honey (Optional):

5. If desired, drizzle honey or maple syrup over the Apple Nachos for extra sweetness.

Finish with Cinnamon:

6. Sprinkle ground cinnamon evenly over the top.

Serve:

7. Serve the Apple Nachos immediately as a delicious and wholesome snack.

Apple Nachos are a versatile snack, and you can customize the toppings based on your preferences. This recipe provides a combination of flavors and textures, making it a satisfying and nutritious treat. Enjoy the sweet and crunchy goodness of these Apple Nachos!

Greek Yogurt with Honey and Berries

Ingredients:

    1 cup Greek yogurt
    1 cup mixed berries (such as strawberries, blueberries, raspberries)
    2 tablespoons honey
    Optional: Granola for added crunch

Instructions:

Prepare the Yogurt and Berries:

    In a bowl or serving dish, scoop out Greek yogurt.
    Wash and prepare the mixed berries.
    Arrange the mixed berries on top of the Greek yogurt.

Drizzle with Honey:

4. Drizzle honey over the Greek yogurt and berries. Adjust the amount of honey based on your sweetness preference.

Optional: Add Granola:

5. If you like, sprinkle granola over the top for added texture and crunch.

Serve:

6. Serve the Greek Yogurt with Honey and Berries immediately.

Enjoy this quick and satisfying snack or breakfast that provides a balance of protein from the Greek yogurt, natural sweetness from the berries, and the rich flavor of honey. It's a versatile dish, and you can customize it with your favorite fruits or additional toppings.